SPORTSMAN'S
BEST
B O O K & D V D S E R I E S

FS Books:

Sportsman's Best: Inshore Fishing
Sportsman's Best: Offshore Fishing
Sportsman's Best: Snapper & Grouper
Sportsman's Best: Sailfish
Sportsman's Best: Redfish
Sportsman's Best: Trout

Sport Fish of Florida
Sport Fish of the Gulf of Mexico
Sport Fish of the Atlantic
Sport Fish of Fresh Water
Sport Fish of the Pacific

Baits, Rigs & Tackle
Annual Fishing Planner
The Angler's Cookbook

Florida Sportsman Magazine
Shallow Water Angler Magazine
Florida Sportsman Fishing Charts
Lawsticks
Law Boatstickers

Author, Terry Gibson
Edited by Terry Gibson and Florida Sportsman Staff
Art Director, Drew Wickstrom
Illustrations by Joe Suroviec
Copy Edited by Sam Hudson
Photos by Scott Sommerlatte, Joe Richard,
Kendall Osborne, David McCleaf and FS Staff

First Printing
Copyright 2008 by Florida Sportsman
InterMedia Outdoors
All Rights Reserved
Printed in the United States of America
ISBN(10) 1-892947-26-9
ISBN(13) 978-1-892947-26-0

www.floridasportsman.com

TROUT

CONTENTS

SB

SPORTSMAN'S BEST
T R O U T

10

44

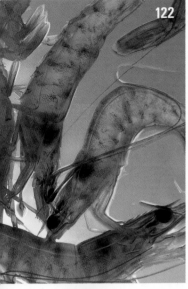

Lifelike plastic shrimp is a proven tool for catching trout, among hundreds of baits and numerous tactics.

The Learning Curve

Trout. Say that word anywhere along the Southeastern Atlantic or Gulf Coast and heads will perk up, because you're not referring to just another fine gamefish, you're talking about an institution. You could say speckled trout if you prefer, or even spotted seatrout, but it won't make your meaning any clearer. Just plain "trout" will do very well, thank you. Trout hold a special place in the hearts of Southern anglers, simply because no other game species is more familiar or more democratic.

If we were somehow afforded the opportunity to design a perfect inshore fish, we could scarcely improve on the trout. Yes, it's true that numerous species from the same waters—redfish and bluefish, for example—put up stronger fights. And it's also true that a few of their fellow fishes—pompano and flounder come to mind—rank higher on the preferred dining list of most seafood lovers. Nevertheless, trout strike hard, wage a showy battle and provide delicious meals.

It's almost too much that trout are also more plentiful than other popular sportfish, and generally eager to swallow any bait or lure tossed their way.

Eager to bite? Then why bother to read this book?

Because, of course, trout are not always such suckers. As cooperative as they may be in many places and under certain conditions, trout are still fish. That means the bigger they get, the more cautious they become; and the more difficult to locate and coax to the end of your line. Any angler who cares to advance beyond the simple tactic of drifting randomly and releasing undersize trout all day long will benefit to no end from this book.

Trout frequent many habitats, from the surf of outside islands to the upper reaches of coastal creeks. They can be caught from piers, bridges and shorelines, as well as from boats. But keeping up with those movements is no easy task. Common belief holds that trout stick to shallow water in spring and summer, then retreat inland to warmer depths in the winter. That is indeed a good rule of thumb, but the fact is that anglers in many areas routinely catch trout—lots of trout—in deeper water all year long. Often enough, the biggest trout will be found in the shallowest water.

Deep. Shallow. Summer. Winter. Surf. Bay. Those are just a few of the problems any trout angler has to wade through, before he even begins to ponder what tackle and lures will best handle a given situation.

Never fear. That is exactly the kind of vital information you will uncover as you turn these pages. Not only has author Terry Gibson become well-steeped in trout lore from his own extensive experience, but he also has taken full advantage of the expert knowledge and research materials available to him as an editor of both *Shallow Water Angler* and *Florida Sportsman* magazines.

So get ready for more consistent action on trout than you've ever enjoyed before.

—Vic Dunaway,
Senior Editor, *Florida Sportsman* Magazine

Cool water, warm summer day, lovely scenery and big trout. No wonder the species is the South's favorite gamefish.

Introduction
Confession of a Trout Fanatic

Forgive me Neptune for I have sinned. Once, in a *Shallow Water Angler* feature article, I maligned the magnificent spotted seatrout (*Cynoscion nebulosus*). Ignoring all other sublime qualities—the heart-stopping topwater assaults, the tasty white meat, widespread availability—a small and petty meanness in me prevailed to point out that once hooked, trout "fight like the French." Penance is for You to set, but I promise to be a sportsman who respects the resources.

In truth, it took a while for me to appreciate seatrout. The first "speck" I ever caught whacked a Johnson Silver Minnow with a white curly grub tail. I was 8 or 9, and on a windy winter day my parents, sister and I were blind casting along the edge of a flat in Everglades National Park. Minutes before, I had landed my first redfish, which had peeled off 100 feet of 10-pound mono so fast compared to the 2-pound trout, which barely bent the flimsy spinning rod. I yammered on about that redfish the whole way home. I don't remember saying much about the trout. Looking back across 25 years of flats fishing, I realize trout are a species many anglers come to appreciate as a gamefish.

Fishing for big trout can become an obsession. The gators I've caught came from the southern Indian River Lagoon, which is two minutes from my house. Around here, trout over 30 inches are considered gators. Once, I bragged about a 28-inch fish in a local bait shop, and a veteran guide scolded me saying, "This is big-girl land—smart big-girl land." Anglers who frequently catch gators deservedly enjoy serious cache. I've caught hundreds of bonefish and tarpon on flies, and submit that sight fishing for gator trout is much more difficult. No matter how you fish for them, big trout are also far more difficult to fool than snook or redfish. And while we're making comparisons, the only thing that whacks a topwater harder than a trout is a snook or a striper. Beyond the challenges inherent in fishing for gators, it's also the relative scarcity of big trout that makes a gator such a memorable catch.

Trout are also great ecological barometers. Highly fecund, large females are capable of generating more than 800,000 eggs every other week during the spawning months. If trout numbers decline suddenly, something is really wrong. For example, in the 1950s and '60s, my dad knew great trout fishing in Florida's Lake Worth Lagoon, where I also grew up. Most of the 75-year-old West Palm Beach Fishing Club's trout records came from that water body. But the species all but disappeared in the filthy lagoon until the state banned gill nets and local authorities employed aggressive water quality improvement strategies and habitat restoration projects. They aren't abundant, but the fact that there is now a viable and improving trout fishery there is a great source of satisfaction for local officials and their supporters in the fishing community. This is the kind of story in which we, as anglers, must continue to be the protagonists.

—Terry Gibson
Projects Editor, *Florida Sportsman Communications Network*

CHAPTER 1

The South's Favorite Fish

According to studies, speckled trout are one of the most commonly targeted inshore species in the Gulf of Mexico. More than 2.9 million fish were landed in 2004. There are many reasons why so many anglers fish for them. They can be challenging to catch (especially big trout), they're good to eat and they are stunning to behold. The yellow mouth, prominent canine(s) and fantastic camouflage also lend them sinister, mysterious aspects that their scientific name, *Cynoscion nebulosus* reflects. It roughly translates "nebulous drum," and refers to the constellations of spots that camouflage this ambush feeder.

Common names for this member of the drum family include speckled trout or "speck," spotted seatrout or seatrout, and yellowmouths. Close relatives include the weakfish (*C. regalis*) and the white trout (*C. arenarius*), but the drum/croaker (*Scianidae*) family is very large. Seatrout are among the largest, most widely distributed and abundant gamefish in that family. Where stocks are managed well and habitat is healthy, bringing home a mess of trout usually isn't too difficult.

Spotted seatrout are evolutionary masterpieces of disguise. There may be bigger, harder-fighting inshore fish, but few hit with such heart-stopping aggression as these ambush feeders.

See DVD for more on the South's favorite fish.

Keen eyesight allows trout to strike with extreme accuracy. One or a pair of long fang teeth help the fish grasp and hold onto prey.

Abundant Fun

The spotted seatrout ranks among the top three of America's most popular inshore gamefish. From south of the border in Holbox, Mexico to the Chesapeake Bay and occasionally northward, they inhabit almost every type of coastal habitat. These habitats include marsh grass, oyster reefs, many species of seagrasses, mangroves, inlets and jetties, sandy beaches and a variety of natural and manmade reefs.

The enormous variety in the places

Trout lurk around enormously varied ambush points. Favorites are marsh points, oyster reefs and potholes.

Kids on summer break chase trout in kayaks. Talk about good, clean fun.

ers, strike aggressively and are downright tasty. And let's not forget that trout fishing is a great way to get kids into fishing, or keep them interested on tough days. That's the most important reason why we need to manage trout harvests and trout habitats sustainably.

Trout fishing can teach anglers young or old a tremendous variety of inshore techniques. Some anglers opt for bobbers and bait. Topwater addicts generally prefer conventional baitcasting rods and reels. The high priests of finesse choose very sensitive graphite spinning rods and braided lines to toss light soft-plastic baits or small sinking plugs, and work them through seagrasses and over structures. When blind casting and/or fishing in deeper water, fly anglers are challenged. But fly anglers have a distinct stealth advantage sight casting in very shallow water where trout are among the most difficult and exciting quarry to hunt with a rod and reel. Because of their dental work and long slender bodies, big trout are called "gators." If you succeed in coaxing a gator into exploding on a fly or light offering, you still have to deal with the headshakes and the fact that trout are adept at spitting hooks.

Specialists in pursuit of heavyweight trout may use premium equipment, but most anglers do fine with whatever they find affordable. A shallow-draft technical flats skiff is handy when sight casting for big gators, but canoes, kayaks, johnboats, bay boats, and even inner tubes, or for that matter bare feet,

where you can catch trout lends to their popularity, as does their wide range and accessibility. You don't have to go far to catch trout; some places you can just wade out from the shoreline. Plus trout are generally very abundant, they're eager feed-

Trout fishing is a family favorite. Fast, steady and reliable action keeps everyone grinning.

Trout will lurk under the shade of mangroves, close to shore. But they also hold near subtle depth changes off the bank. It's best to work your way in slowly.

The definition of a "gator" seatrout varies by region. They grow bigger in some

can put you on trout in many places. A few diehard surf anglers build tricked-out beach buggies to chase trout in the suds.

Before you go out and buy the best tackle and boat to catch trout, learn about the area or areas you intend to fish most. The biggest seatrout are commonly caught only in relatively specific areas, such as Florida's Indian River and Mosquito lagoons, Sabine Lake on the Texas/Louisiana border, and Texas' Lower Laguna Madre. Other places in Texas and Mexico have big trout, and they catch a few gators up in the sounds of North Carolina. But in Georgia, South Carolina and most of the Central Gulf coast, specks are limited in growth by a number of environmental factors. They're quite common, even a dominant species in those areas. But they rarely exceed 24 inches and are treated mostly as a panfish. Very

light tackle makes these tasty fish more fun to catch.

If you know where to fish and have decent fishing skills, you can catch trout throughout most of their range year round. Spotted seatrout have flourished for a long time, about 60 million years, and to last that long a species must be well adapted to extreme environmental changes. These include an incredible tolerance for huge swings in water temperatures. In summer, the best fishing will almost always take place early, late and in the dark. In winter, the bite most often occurs midafternoon, when the shallows are starting to warm. But if the shallows get too hot or too cold, trout simply find deeper holes or channels. You can just about always coax a few to bite if you work a bait or scented soft plastic slowly enough.

drift. If you shine it, trout will come.

The "crappie lights" aren't the only page to come out of freshwater playbooks. A strong argument can be made that most of the refinements in inshore saltwater fishing throughout the past 20 years were influenced, if not outright borrowed, from freshwater fishing. Trout feed much like black bass, walleye and crappie. Part of the reason the species is still increasing in popularity is because so many Americans are moving from the interior to coastal areas. Many of these folks liked to fish for freshwater fish, and they find that besides abundance, availability and good eats, fishing tactics for trout really aren't much different, just a little more exciting.

Take the venerable wobbling, weedless spoon. Bass anglers have been swimming those through lily pads for more than a century. Spoon tactics were quickly adopted as inshore saltwater recreational fishing was pioneered in the 20th century. Hair

areas than in others.

Trout feed day and night, but they tend to feed most vigorously in low-light conditions or in the dark. They'll flock to dock lights and bridge lights, which attract baitfish, shrimp and other forage. In fact, in mid-Atlantic waters, many of the really large weakfish (the spotted seatrout's often larger cousin) are taken at night around lighted docks and bridges. In Texas, and there's no reason why this won't work elsewhere, some anglers take a page from the crappie playbook and rig up an array of lights around the boat. You can anchor or

Day or night, you can catch trout. At night, the fish hang around dock lights. Low-amperage, fluorescent green lights really attract them.

bugs, walking, sinking and diving plugs, as well as soft-plastic baits also came from freshwater fishing. If you've fished much in fresh water, or for other saltwater species inshore, you may know more about how to catch spotted seatrout than you realize. **SB**

CHAPTER 2

The Spotted Seatrout

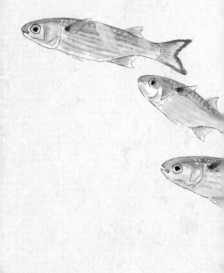

Beyond its popularity as a gamefish, the spotted seatrout is one of the most intriguing members in the very large family of fishes, *Sciaenidae*. Common names include "speckled trout," "speck," "seatrout" or just plain "trout." Their scientific name, *Cynoscion nebulosus*, means roughly, "nebulous drum." Although in the name of good management we can never understand enough about such a valuable gamefish, there is very little about this fish that remains shrouded in mystery.

The Sciaenid family is also very old, about 60 million years. They are "spiny ray fishes," and it is thought that they evolved from the earliest relatives of striped bass and snook. The seatrout's range is limited to the Gulf of Mexico to the mid-Atlantic waters of the Chesapeake Bay. Throughout most of their normal range, they cohabit with close relatives, including the black drum (*Pagonias cromis*), whiting (*Menticirrhus americanus*), various croakers, red drum (*Sciaenops ocellatus*), spot (*Leiostomus xanthurus*) and white trout (*Cynoscion arenarius*). From Jacksonville, Florida, north to the Chesapeake Bay, spotted seatrout also overlap with their larger, more migratory cousin, the weakfish (*Cynoscion regalis*).

Like most drum species, seatrout are limited to tropical temperate waters. They have been documented as far north as Cape Cod.

Jason Mathias
Pair of spotted seatrout
feeding on favorite forage,
finger mullet.

Life History

Scientists use the term "life history" to describe the reproductive cycles of plants and animals. The life history of spotted seatrout is well understood, and like most gamefish, they usually prefer a variety of inshore and in some regions offshore habitats at different sizes.

Spawning

Throughout most of the spotted seatrout's range, spawning takes place from early April until late October. Spawning often gets started later in the spring toward the northern end of the species' range, such as the Chesapeake Bay. Anglers often say the month or so leading up to the spawn is the best time to target trophy trout. The production of gametes requires an enormous amount of energy, and seatrout produce an incredible amount of gametes. A mature female can

Both male and female trout have organs to generate sound, but only the males actually "talk."

produce over a million eggs every two weeks. So, big trout feed more voraciously and recklessly late winter/early spring in preparation for the spawn. Interestingly, neither the smaller males nor the females feed during the spawn itself, which is a tremendous advantage for the species' survival. The spawn usually occurs at sundown and feeding usually occurs afterward but well after most anglers have gone home.

Scientists have documented two peaks in the spawning season for trout in Tampa Bay, Florida: One around the full moon of May or June, and another during a late summer full moon. It is assumed that in terms of seasonality and lunar phases, similar spawning peaks occur throughout the range and that spawning usually occurs twice a month (around the new and full moons) throughout the spawning season. Counts of juvenile trout in South Carolina peak in September, which gives support to the peak-spawning assumptions. In Louisiana, researchers have documented aggregations where spawning resumes only 7 days after the previous spawning event.

Much of what we know about trout spawning and the things that can interfere with the spawn is from Dr. Grant

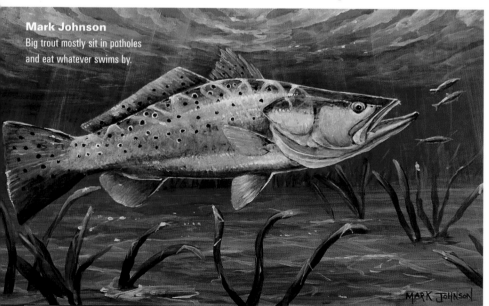

Mark Johnson
Big trout mostly sit in potholes and eat whatever swims by.

Guy Harvey

Trout aren't big jumpers, but surface flies and lures encourage fish to leap out of the water on occasion.

Spotted Seatrout

Gilmore's research on Florida's famous Indian River Lagoon, and from scientists building on his research elsewhere. Gilmore was the first scientist to describe the more than 800 fish species found in the Indian River Lagoon and the rivers that flow into it, establishing the estuary as North America's most biologically diverse. Taking a page out of the cetacean (whale/dolphin) research playbook, Gilmore pioneered the use of acoustic monitoring to study fishes. Acoustic monitoring uses an underwater microphone called a hydrophone to record fish sounds. The Florida Fish & Wildlife Research Institute (FWRI) is enamored with this

Acoustic telemetry is an exciting advance in technology. Hydrophones are used to record fish movements and behavior.

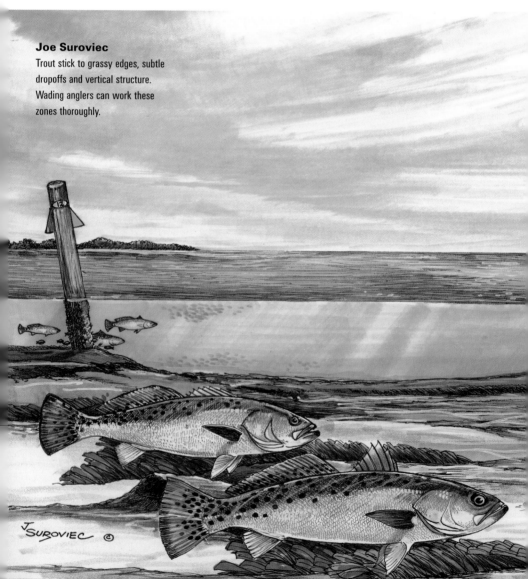

Joe Suroviec
Trout stick to grassy edges, subtle dropoffs and vertical structure. Wading anglers can work these zones thoroughly.

technique because, Gilmore says, "Scientists can learn about where and when fish spawn without having to disrupt spawning or sacrifice fish."

Gilmore's acoustic research has dispelled Cousteau's notion of the "silent" undersea world. Some fish make quite a racket, especially the species in the Sciaenid (drum) clan. The sounds they make have distinct sonic signatures, so it's easy to tell who's making all the noise, and where.

Among most drum species, only the male drum can call. Male trout make use of an extrinsic sonic muscle that runs along either side of the swim bladder, the organ that allows fish to maintain a vertical position in the water column. Muscles manipulate the swim bladder to make the croaking sound you hear when you handle a male trout. Since sound waves travel much farther through water than air (1,500 meters/sec to about 340 meters/sec), this vocal ability is a tremendous

advantage in terms of attracting females. Because water traps sound, we can't hear the cacophony above water. But wade through a spawning aggregation and you can feel the noise vibrations on your feet and legs. Float over an aggregation, and you can hear the chorus if you put your ear to the hull.

Prior to the spawn, environmental cues such as rising water temps and lengthening days trigger growth in the extrinsic muscles and

Trout expend a tremendous amount of energy during spawning. It's easiest to catch them during the pre-spawn gorge.

increased circulatory ability in the blood vessels that supply them with oxygen. Muscles get tuna-blood red from use. Likewise, as spawning season approaches, the size of the females' ovaries increase.

Although it would seem that males would have a better chance of successfully fertilizing a female's eggs with fewer competitors around, scientists think that males gather in large drumming aggregations to add voices to the chorus. The greater number of voices enhances the volume of the chorus and thus extends the range of the mating call. More girls get the word. You can listen to a

Randy McGovern
The most exciting way to fish for trout is with surface lures and flies. A trout lunges from the grass to whack a walking plug.

Randy ©07
McGovern

Helterskeletons.com
Seatrout physiology has perfectly
evolved for ambush feeding.

Understanding the seatrout's habitat preferences can help you protect the

recording of the trout mating call at http://research.myfwc.com/features/view_article.asp?id=26398.

Males start calling just before sundown and have been recorded calling for 3 to 12 hours, according to FWRI researchers. It is thought that spawning occurs around dusk because most planktivores aren't as active in the darkness. Predation isn't as much of a factor for the fertilized eggs. Still, less than one percent of the fertilized eggs will survive to sexual maturity.

Trout are loyal to specific aggregation areas, generally areas where currents will widely disperse eggs. Tampa Bay researchers have found that areas characterized by seagrass bordering a sharp depth change are frequently used by spotted seatrout for spawning.

Site preferences change from water body to water body. In Florida's Indian River Lagoon, trout exhibit a strong

species and catch more fish.

that can influence trout spawning are salinity, water quality and noise. Salinity seems to be the most important factor. Most spawning occurs in water between 14 and 23 parts salt per thousand.

Eggs, Larvae and Juveniles

Fertilized eggs float along on the whims of currents. Unfertilized eggs sink and become food for crabs and other benthic (bottom-dwelling) organisms. Trout eggs hatch within 24 to 36 hours; salinity levels affect the rate of embryonic development. Saltier water causes the yolk to be depleted more quickly. Yolk depletion is a good thing, because upon depletion the egg hatches. The ability to hatch quickly is a selective advantage because larvae have tails and some ability to escape predators.

Larvae quickly drop to the bottom, to find cover. During this period, they feed primarily on other plankton. Next they morph into their post-larval form, a translucent fish about 3 mm long. In the mangrove and seagrass-rich waters of Florida and Texas, newly settled trout are most commonly found on a margin of seagrass and sand. Juvenile trout in Florida will also settle on oyster reefs and in mangrove creeks. North and northwest of the mangrove line, newly settled trout find refuge and food in shallow spartina-lined creeks, around oyster reefs and in marsh grasses. Along the central Gulf Coast, newly settled trout have also been documented out on the continental shelf, hiding in mud or modest pieces of structure.

Newly settled trout feed primarily on microscopic animals and then change to slightly larger animals called copepods and amphipods. As size, strength and swimming speed increase, the diet shifts to larger forage such as opossum shrimp or even grass shrimp. As seatrout grow, baitfish, especially mud minnows where trout have settled in creeks, become increasingly important dietary components.

At about 3 months, once the juveniles reach 6 or 7 inches, young trout abandon their nursery habitats and venture out into the estuary where they form schools of simi-

degree of loyalty to specific grassflats along the 120-mile water body. In Louisiana, both drumming aggregations and spawning take place in areas 6 to 16 feet deep with good tidal flow, such as passes and channels. But researchers have found that in many places trout spawning aggregations are highly varied. One Louisiana study found that environmental conditions were more important than places. Some environmental conditions

Jim Roberts

A trout's skin is a camouflage veil that changes according to light, water and bottom color.

lar-sized fish. At this point they are fully oscillated, or spotted. They've put on camouflage. Trout mature sexually within a year, which is a huge advantage over slow-growing fish such as groupers, which too often are harvested before they get a chance to reproduce. Females grow much more quickly and much larger than males, and the female's ability to produce eggs is directly proportionate to her size. Spotted seatrout can live up to 10 years and possibly longer, achieving sizes of greater than 15 pounds.

Adult Habitats

A good understanding of trout habitat preferences will increase your fishing success. These include seagrass flats, mud flats, mangrove shorelines, oyster reefs, marshlands and bay areas, coastal rivers, beaches, shoals, offshore live bottom and every kind of manmade structure imaginable. An intimate understanding of the individual habitats that occur where you fish is essential to being at the right place at the right time and fishing with the most productive bait, lure or fly.

Throughout their range, a general seasonal migration occurs from open-water areas in bays, sounds and lagoons in the summer months, to the confines of chan-

nels and creeks in the winter. November is the month when trout migrate, but the timing of this migration depends on salinity, water temperature and bait. Heavy winter rains can ruin trout fishing far up central Gulf Coast rivers, Low Country creeks and North Carolina creeks. Baitfish runs such as the mullet run along the Atlantic seaboard also draw trout out of protected waters and into the surf zone.

While the nature of the habitat is an important consideration, the nature of the fish is equally important to think about when you're deciding where to cast. While most drums are foragers, trout are vicious ambushers.

In fact, owing to the species' prominent

Ted Baker

This September, 1975 cover of *Florida Sportsman,* a Ted Baker original, elevated the question, how do trout miss all those treble hooks? When fishing topwaters let the trout hook itself. Just reel down and keep the line taut.

canine or canines, the etymology of the spotted seatrout's scientific name means something like "nebulous, dog-like sea fish." A small depression or pothole in a flat or cluster of oysters is all the setup this ambusher needs.

Trout have incredible confidence in their camouflage and will lie still until the boat or wader is virtually on top them. They can even enhance the effectiveness of their camouflage by controlling a melanin-concentrating hormone. (Melanin is the same chemical that causes skin to turn brown when exposed to the sun.) In tannin-stained waters they can "put on" a coppery sheen. In clear ocean water, they pale to a silver sheen and even their spots look diluted. They're so good at hiding, that sight fishing for trout can downright strain your corneas.

Trout have remarkable eyesight and a keen sense of smell as well as a keen ability to detect vibration. But, trout won't travel far for a meal. Instead, they're likely to eye a meal for some time, or react violently to the sudden appearance of food. Hence, presentation is everything. Well almost everything. Matching the hatch can be important. Bigger trout tend to be more pisciverous, and big baits, flies and lures catch big trout. Mullet, menhaden, croakers, pilchards, pinfish, pigfish and

sand perch are common forage. But shrimp runs get them keyed in on crustaceans and even the biggest, most jaded trout of the Indian River Lagoon fall for shrimp or crab imitations. Keep in mind that trout prefer things that look slow and crippled, or that dart at an angle away from the fish's eye.

Although not as visibly a schooling fish as most drums, such as red drum, trout are hardly loners. Catch one schoolie fish and you'll likely find many more in the area. Since trout tend to regurgitate when excited or while feeding intensely, the oils from partially digested food rise to the surface to make a slick. Some say the odor

© flying
fisherman

resembles bubble gum, watermelon or freshly mowed grass.

Because they are so often seen lying alone in potholes, big female trout often give the illusion of being loners. They are much more independent than smaller trout and the males in general. However, if you spook a gator, don't assume that's the only big trout around. Big trout tend to stack up on the same flat in good numbers, but give each other a certain amount of space. Others are probably within casting range.

Predators

The number of predators directly decreases in proportion to a trout's age and size. As embryos and larval beings, trout are vulnerable to every imaginable filter feeder and a host of other slightly older fish species. Birds and a wide variety of predator fish, from blennies to bigger trout, feed on newly settled, early juvenile and juvenile trout. Quite a bit of cannibalism occurs even on nearly mature juveniles. Large gamefish such as snook, striped bass, barracuda and bluefish may feed on smaller trout, and 'cudas, sharks and porpoises will feed on trout regardless of size. But as trout grow, they become some of the most formidable predators in the shallow-water world.

In some areas, Pavlovian porpoises now follow anglers around and feed on tired trout that anglers throw back. Ultimately however, human beings are the trout's most significant predator. Pollution and habitat destruction can remove entire year classes. Gill-netting can wipe out an entire spawning aggregation. And overfishing, especially killing the large breeder females which make up the minority of the stock, can stunt and diminish local populations. As pressure increases, anglers will need to be more conscientious and self-regulating than ever to assure viable populations of spotted seatrout.

Weakfish and Other Trouts

Spotted seatrout belong to a very large family of fishes that comprises the world's many drums and croakers. Some species of drum, such as the reef-dwelling high hat (*Equetus*

and back of this fish is dark brown in color with a sublime greenish tinge. The sides have a faint silvery hue with dusky specks and the belly is white. The common name is not meant to be condescending. They actually fight pretty well,

It is thought that some hybridization occur

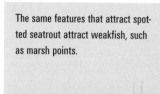

The same features that attract spotted seatrout attract weakfish, such as marsh points.

acuminatus) occur in the same range but not in the same habitats, so they rarely if ever cross paths with the spotted seatrout. In fact, many drum species have very little in common with their cousin the spotted seatrout. But three closely related species co-occur with the spotted seatrout and are often caught while fishing for seatrout. These are the weakfish (*Cynoscion regalis*), the white trout (*Cynoscion arenarius*) and the silver seatrout (*Cynoscion nothus*).

Weakfish

Also called gray trout, weakfish occur from Nova Scotia to northeast Florida but are most abundant from North Carolina through Long Island Sound. It is the state fish of Delaware.

The "regal" trout comes by its scientific name "*C regalis*" honestly. The head

relatively speaking. Weakfish are called as much because their mouth muscles are so soft that hooks often tear free.

Although not considered overfished, dramatic fluctuations in year-class population sizes make weakfish fisheries unpredictable. They are somewhat elusive, a novelty among anglers, especially in the Northeast where the inshore recreational fishery is basically limited to bluefish and striped bass. A subset of anglers target weakfish very seriously

between trout species, possibly even between weakfish and spotted seatrout.

Weakfish can get significantly larger on average than most spotted seatrout. Flyfishing techniques for either species are similar.

with fly and light tackle, in very shallow water, using tactics similar to what works for big speckled trout. Like trout, weakfish will hit a variety of jigs, plugs, flies, lures and baits. They are excellent tablefare, but many anglers, having watched them come and go, have sworn off killing weakfish.

Weakfish get significantly bigger than speckled trout and generally are bigger where the species cross range boundaries. The current record is a tie at 19.2 pounds. One fish was caught at Jones Beach, NY, in 1984; the other in Delaware Bay in 1989.

Adult weakfish are associated with a wide variety of habitats, but eelgrass is a favorite and the marshes of Delaware and New Jersey hold plenty of fish. Oyster reefs, rips, docks, jetties and live bottom are also common haunts. In the fall, adult weakfish begin an offshore and southerly migration to the continental shelf from the Chesapeake Bay to Cape Lookout, North Carolina where they overwinter on nearshore reefs and wrecks. SB

The shallow reefs off southern North Carolina are great places to catch large weakfish.

Weakfish, left, has linear pattern of much smaller, more numerous spots than the spotted seatrout at right. Florida has closed seasons on spotted seatrout that vary from region to region. Weakfish are fair game year-round, but be careful not to mistake the two.

Sand Trout

Also called the "white trout," the sand trout is a Gulf species that may occur in the Atlantic waters of extreme southeastern Florida. Adults are predominantly found inshore residing in bays and inlets but may move offshore during winter or summer months. Seasonally, large sand seatrout will congregate at offshore oil and gas platforms in moderately shallow water depths. Sand trout rarely exceed 1 pound or 10 to 12 inches, but fish between 3 and 5 pounds can be caught in deep inshore holes and in offshore waters.

A sand trout's body is silver, with a yellow cast above and yellowish fins. When sand seatrout grow larger than a pound, they develop a beautiful iridescent lavender cast on their heads and the front part of their bodies. One or two prominent canine teeth are set usually at the tip of the upper jaw inside a yellow mouth. Sand seatrout eat fishes and shrimp, but they are rated as the number one shrimp predator in the Gulf of Mexico.

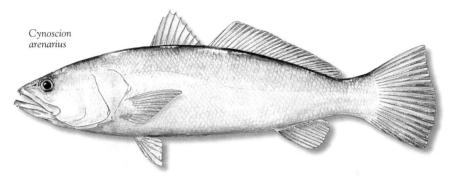

Cynoscion arenarius

Silver Seatrout

Silver seatrout are the smallest seatrout, rarely growing larger than a ½ pound or 10 to 12 inches. They are pale straw colored above, with silvery sides and a white belly. They have no distinctive pigmentation, although faint diagonal lines may be present on the back and shoulders. The silver seatrout is entirely silver without any of the yellow coloration on the back and fins that the sand seatrout has. The silver trout also has very small, darker spots arranged in rearward sloping rows or the upper sides.

Like other seatrouts, they sport one or two prominent canine teeth at the tip of the upper jaw. One clue to distinguish them is that the lower half of the tail is longer than the upper half. Silver trout are most common over sand or sandy mud bottoms offshore along both the Gulf and Atlantic coasts of Florida and are especially abundant in the northern Gulf of Mexico. They migrate into bays during cold months, where they are caught by anglers fishing for their larger cousins. **SB**

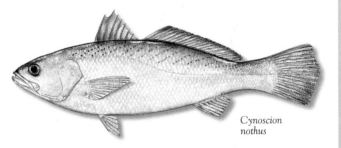

Cynoscion nothus

CHAPTER 3

Mainstay Fishery

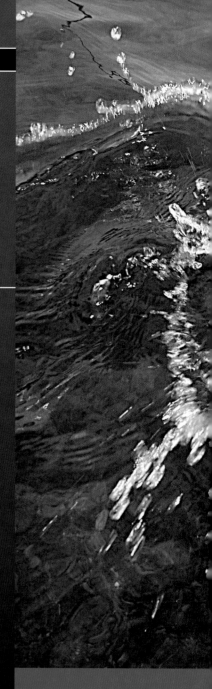

Trout fishing means many things to diverse types of anglers, including trophy fish and personal bests, topwater action, stoked kids, and a mess of fish to fry. A day of redfishing or snook fishing can easily become the day that trophy trout hopped on the line unanticipated, or about a happy school of fish that provided too consistent action to leave. We love trout and are always happy to see them, most importantly because healthy trout populations are a good sign of a healthy ecosystem.

As discussed in Chapter 2, spotted seatrout are an incredibly fecund species. If the fishery is managed well, stocks can hold up to heavy pressure. When management decisions are at hand, managers are supposed to remember that the "fishery" comprises the stock, the essential habitats and water quality, and the communities that fish for the individual species. Some states, including Alabama, South Carolina and Texas, have had the wisdom to give seatrout "gamefish status," a designation which makes it illegal to sell trout.

Study upon study has shown tremendous ecological and economic benefit when important species are protected from commercial exploitation.

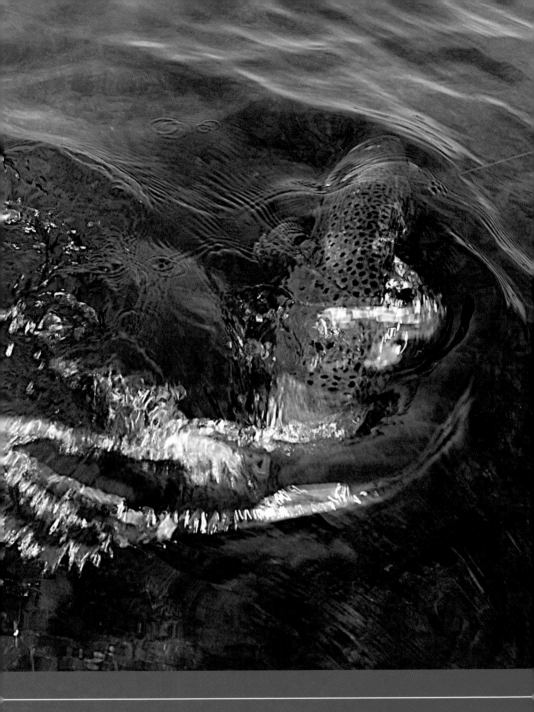

Wherever you find seagrass flats, you'll probably find seatrout. They spend most of their lives in the grassy shallows.

All-American Favorites

Anglers need to be stewards of the resource. We need to challenge managers to enforce sustainable limits and protect habitats.

Some use the word "staple" to describe the importance of spotted seatrout to America's fishing communities. Trout were most certainly a vital food staple for Florida pioneers and for 19th and 20th century coastal communities throughout the species' range. Today, trout have very little subsistence or commercial significance. In describing the modern fishery, the nautical definition of "mainstay" seems more apropos. A mainstay is a strong rope that serves to steady the main mast of a sailing vessel. From Texas to the Chesapeake Bay, trout fishing keeps inshore recreational fishing communities sailing right along.

Although trout don't get the televised fanfare of a tournament series devoted to them, folks are very passionate about and grateful for trout. The Texas Parks and Wildlife Department reports that close to 1.5 million people participate in saltwater fishing each year, and 75 percent of them pursued trout some or all of the time. The Atlantic States Fisheries Management Council (ASFMC) recognizes that in Florida, trout are often the most sought-after inshore species. The Georgia Department of Natural Resources Coastal Resources Division estimates that recreational fishing for trout generates $20 to $40 million annually. And National Marine Fisheries Service data show that seatrout are always among the top ten most popular species targeted in their range, and they are considered the most sought-after species in the Gulf of Mexico.

Watch those trebles! The best way to grab a hooked trout is to pinch the fish with two fingers right behind the upper gill plates.

Trophy Hunters

The quest for trophy trout drives much of this enthusiasm. In some areas, gator trout are a lifelong pursuit for many anglers. Southeast Texas is one of the top big-trout regions, and trout fishing gets downright

You don't need a fancy boat to catch trout. In fact, stealth modes such as kayaking and wading more often lead to catches like this big fish.

competitive. Every trip, these trout fanatics are trying to top their personal best fish, and everyone else's.

"The sight fishing for redfish thing has really caught on in Texas, and I really enjoy it," said Capt. Brandon Shuler, of Port Mansfield. "But around here anglers are judged more by their ability to consistently catch big trout."

Trout tournaments are serious business in Texas. The Gulf Coast Troutmasters Association is the state's most prestigious

Family Favorites Trout fishing will often hold a young angler's in

Father and son work a shoreline dropoff on a cool day. Youngster wisely wears an automatically inflating life vest. Right, clearly a priceless outing.

tournament series, and many top guides have cemented their reputations by winning these tournaments. Other states have big events, too. The Coastal Conservation Association's S.T.A.R. Tournament, two of of the largest and most lucrative tournaments in Texas and Louisiana, have speckled trout divisions. Small local tournaments are regularly held from Texas to Virginia. In Texas and along the Central Gulf Coast, corporate culture becomes fishing culture as it is popular to send employees to the coast for a weekend's fishing and impromptu tournament.

Gator trout also have a way of putting sleepy

onger than the bigger, savvier inshore species.

Trout fishing is all about action and family fun. There isn't a more classic sight in inshore fishing than a dad anchored up on an oyster reef or drifting a flat while trout tug down popping corks and kids tug on trout. Because lots of simple techniques work, trout fishing is one of the best ways to introduce kids to fishing. And then the kids can go home proud with a mess of fish.

Trout fishing can be as simple as a jig and a light spinning rod. Floats, soft plastics and trout are a proven combo that has saved the day on many an inshore fishing trip. But anglers can learn to employ much more sophisticated approaches, from walking topwater plugs to making long casts with fly tackle. Trout fishing can teach you just about the entire spectrum of inshore techniques.

Trout allow you to be a fair- and foul-weather angler. There's no excuse for staying home. Trout can be caught almost regardless of how extreme heat, cold and wind. It has to be absolutely rank cold and honking or HOT not to catch trout. Even then, you can probably find some fish in deep holes. Sure beats watching TV. SB

places on the map. Port Mansfield, Texas may be a nondescript stop on the Texas coast, but this south Texas town is the gateway to the Lower Laguna Madre (LLM), North America's only hypersaline lagoon. The LLM's unique ecology produces arguably more giants than any other trout-producing system. Every year, the Port Mansfield Chamber of Commerce holds a tournament to promote this fascinating fishery as a destination.

Lake Calcasieu, which straddles the Texas

Louisiana border, is the most famous gator trout destination in the northern Gulf. The oyster reefs are the draw for trout, but the fish sometimes venture out along the beaches.

Gator trout are also one of Jensen Beach, Florida's claims to fame. Jensen Beach sits on a peninsula separating the Indian River Lagoon (IRL) and St. Lucie River, North America's most biologically diverse estuaries. The sheer biomass that these estuaries produce is almost unquantifiable. Suffice to say that trout never lack for a hearty meal, and the warm weather keeps them feeding and growing year-round. This is the area where Mark Nichols field tests and refines his revolutionary soft-plastic lures, such as the D.O.A. Shrimp. Although snook, reds and other species are abundant in the southern IRL and St. Lucie, Nichols said he knows he's most onto something when his lures fool big trout consistently.

"They're just so much smarter than everything else," he says.

Topwater Fix

Trout may not be the hardest fighting fish in the estuarine world, but they slam topwaters as readily and as viciously as any other inshore species. That's one of the main reasons why so many anglers target trout trip after trip. The explosion, especially at O dark 30 before the coffee's taken effect, is powerful enough to give a young angler an early heart attack.

"I've been catchin' trout on topwaters

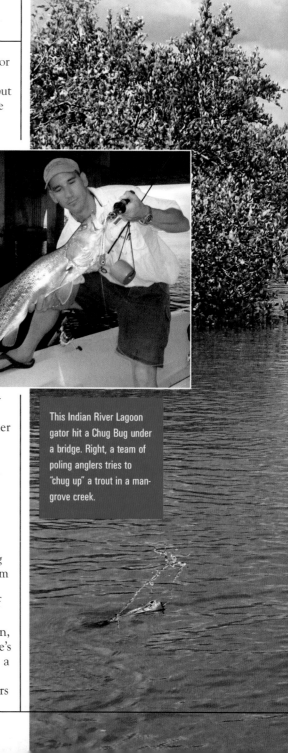

This Indian River Lagoon gator hit a Chug Bug under a bridge. Right, a team of poling anglers tries to "chug up" a trout in a mangrove creek.

Trout don't have the vertical leap of a ladyfish or tarpon, but they can get some air. Give a little slack when they're up and head shaking, but otherwise keep the line tight.

since the '60s," says Lower Laguna Madre Capt. Bruce Shuler, "and I still gotta get my fix."

The fascination with topwater fishing for trout led to the development of classic lures. For example, *Shallow Water Angler* Texas regional editor Scott Sommerlatte works the water column with a wide variety of lures and flies. But when it comes to topwater trout, he goes to the classic Cotton Cordell Broken Back Red Fin.

"It's the original Texas topwater lure," he gushes. Indeed, a lot of classic lures catch trout, and lure collecting has become a serious sidebar for nostalgic anglers.

Some topwater devotees will keep walking the dog or popping that Chug Bug even when the sun is high and anglers fishing subsurface around them are slaying fish. The bite number and hookup ratios may be much lower, but the reward in terms of sheer excitement is worth the work and patience. SB

Trout strike topwater plugs so hard it makes you reluctant to put the plug down and go subsurface when the time comes.

Boating From design innovations

The popularity of trout fishing led to the invention of a very important genre of shallow-water skiffs in Texas and to a lesser degree in the waters of the northern Gulf of Mexico. Texans such as Willis Hudson (Falcon Boats) were among the first boat builders in America to manufacture fiberglass hulls. Decades ago, Hudson and other pioneers developed a special catamaran hull that allows a fairly big skiff to run in only a few

Small armada of bay boats waiting on a tide change. This genre of shallow-running center console is the most popular vessel among trout anglers.

Large, sensitive eyes and a hooked fang or fangs make a trout a frightfully efficient predator.

inches of water. They're called "tunnel hulls" or "scooter boats," and are perfect for taxiing a group of wader-clad anglers from flat to flat, to participate in the time-honored Texas tradition of inline wading.

Through the 1960s, Miami and Florida Keys anglers whittled away at shallow-draft fiberglass runabouts until the classic poling skiff took shape in the form of the Hewes Bonefisher. Descendants of these versatile little boats have been adopted by countless trout anglers.

Elsewhere, flat-bottom johnboats and fiberglass skiffs commonly used by commercial fishermen were adapted to recreational needs. More evolution took place, and in the '90s the "bay boat" emerged. The bay boat is arguably the best choice for the family-minded inshore angler. Today, the most popular bay boats come with options that help make the family fishing trip comfortable and fun. SB

CHAPTER 4

Trout Tackle

A wide range of conventional rods and reels, spinning outfits and fly outfits work well for trout fishing. If you've got it in your rod locker you can probably catch a trout on it. In places, some folks still catch them on cane poles or handlines.

Lure weight and type, and size of fish are the most important considerations in rod and reel selection. You need a lighter rod with more flex when fishing with light soft-plastic lures or light live baits; a light offering just can't load a heavy rod. And it's harder to use a conventional reel, a.k.a. "baitcasting" or "plugcasting" reel, with light lures. Light lures just don't generate the velocity to make the spool revolve easily, so casting distance is limited and backlashes are even more of a problem. Most anglers who fish light offerings prefer spinning tackle for those applications. Conversely, heavy jigs, plugs and spoons feel unwieldy on tackle that is too light, and the rod may not have the backbone to set the hook.

Trout are one of the best species to target when introducing kids or novice anglers to fishing. Light spinning tackle is far and away the most versatile type of fishing gear.

See DVD for more on choosing the right trout tackle.

Fly fishing is deadly effective in tranquil conditions. Above, plug rods and reels and spinning reels are less challenging but more versatile and popular.

Tackle Tips

L earning new skills and techniques is as much a part of the fun as actually catching fish, and seatrout fishing gives you the opportunity to master all three types of tackle commonly used in

Spinning rods, plug rods, fly rods . . . even cane poles and handlines in some

inshore fishing, including plug tackle, spinning tackle and fly tackle. You also get to play with a tremendous assortment of lines, lures, hooks and other gadgets. And if you want to fish with bait, learning to "pancake" a castnet properly is a prerequisite if you want a well full of silver.

A good castnet is necessary, and proper net maintenance ensures that it opens properly and remains pliant.

fisheries . . . have their place in a trout angler's quiver.

Anglers ply a flat with spinning and plug gear. Top right, fly rods and plug rods are often preferred for topwater work. Right, even for jig fishing most Texas trout addicts prefer the revolving reel.

Spinning Gear

Versatile and easy to use, spinning rods work in any trout-fishing situation.

Spinning reels are great for beginners, but experts prefer them for a variety of applications. Some types of trout fishing require finessing light lures, such as soft-plastic shrimp and jerkbaits. You just can't get the distance with a plug reel, and if you're casting a light lure into wind with a revolving reel you're asking for a bad backlash. Another advantage is that most spinning reels are easy to convert to right- or left-hand retrieve. Spinning tackle is simply the most versatile tackle.

Spinning Reels

Reels with revolving spools are formally called "conventional" reels, but in the past 20 years or so spinning tackle has become far and away the most popular, even "conventional" tackle for trout and many other inshore species. In reality, the spinning rod/reel's rise to popularity has taken a half century. Spinning tackle emerged after World War II, and the fixed-spool reels were embraced by the populace. But experienced anglers grew frustrated with the mechanical failures common in the earlier iterations of this complex type of reel, especially in saltwater environments. Although contemporary spinning reels are made from light, strong and very reliable materials such as aluminum and graphite, a waning mistrust lingers among old-timers and in cultural pockets. These days, the mistrust is largely unwarranted.

Specially treated stainless steel ball bearings resist corrosion, while new synthetic drag washers last longer. Larger and longer reel spools and more stainless steel ball bearings improved line capacity, line management and casting distance. Drags are silk smooth.

Spinning tackle excels over casting tackle when fishing light lures or baits and when fishing into the wind. This is especially true when skip-casting baits under overhanging structure. There are more or less four opposing forces when fishing into a headwind with spinning tackle, wind versus the combined resistance and synergized torque of the lure, line and flexed rod. It just doesn't take as much force to make line fly off of a fixed spool as it does a revolving spool. Therefore, spinning tackle will perform better and is the least likely to cause problems when casting light lures into the wind.

When matching a reel to a rod, balance

A new generation of spinning reel offers a wide spool rather than standard long-nose spinning reels. Some anglers say the larger diameter spools offer better line management and greater casting distance.

Leave enough line outside the rodtip for your partner to handle a big, angry trout at boatside.

Vertical rod holders keep spinners ready with lures that cover the water column.

is the most important consideration. You don't want a heavy rod and light reel or a winch on a light rod. You don't need miles of line or heavy line for trout fishing, so go with the lightest reels that still make sense for saltwater applications. Small-diameter braided lines allow anglers to use much smaller, lighter spinning reels than ever before, when we were limited to monofilament. You can easily pack a few hundred yards of 8- or 10-pound braid on a small spinning reel. No trout will ever pull more than 30 yards of line and even 30 yards would be a remarkable run. But where there's trout there may be snook, redfish and other runners.

Alas, manufacturers have not agreed on a universal size system for spinning reels. Generally speaking, an 8-pound-class spinning reel matches the short wading rods and your medium-fast-action rods. A 12-pound-class reel matches slightly heavier fast-action rods.

Spinning Rods

Quality spinning rods are built from strong, sensitive and light high-modulus graphite blanks. Some companies also make rods constructed with a combination of graphite and glass. Special resins bond the two materials, which provide added strength in a fairly light rod. If you plan on doing more bait fishing than finesse fishing, these "hybrids" make sense. While they may not be as sensitive as 100-percent graphite rods, they aren't as expensive and they last longer. Because they don't break easily, these graphite/glass combos are great rods for kids.

Most spinning rods used for shallow-water fishing are between seven and eight feet long. However, some companies offer 6- to 6½-foot rods with short butts for those who like to wade chest deep, and for working overhanging structure such as docks and mangroves. In fact, only in recent years have manufacturers built spinning rods with wading anglers in mind. Most wade fishing was traditionally accomplished with plug tackle, so the new short-handled spinners signal a shift in preference. Most inshore rods are designed to cast lures weighing from ⅛ to 1¼ ounces, and are rated for 8- to 20-pound-test lines. Lure and line ratings are important, but flex, or action, is the most important consideration.

A rod with a fast flex is very stiff. It has a stout butt section, which is ideal for fighting large trout and making long casts. The middle third of the rod is also stiff, with the flexible section located in the upper quarter. There may be a little wiggle in the tip, but not much.

Fast-flex rods punch lures through strong winds, plus they offer a more direct connection to the lure. When fishing jigs in seagrass, they help pop the lure out of the grass and up through the water column with less chance of grass catching on the hook. They drive hooks through plastic and into jaws much more powerfully than "softer" rods. Sensitivity is another attribute. Finally, they're great for short-range work and for skip-casting under mangroves and docks. The added stiffness also helps you land more fish in high-hazard zones.

Two-handed casting is the best way to get distance, an important factor when targeting gator trout. The handle acts as a fulcrum to load the rod deeply.

GUIDE'S PICK SPINNING
Captain Brandon Barlow, Titusville, FL

Rod
- 7-foot 7-inch G Loomis Bronze Back with extra fast tip

Reel
- Shimano Stella 3000

Line
- Spiderwire Ultra Cast clear, 10-pound test

Leader
- 12-pound fluorocarbon

A medium-fast rod wiggles into the upper third of the blank. Because of increased parabolic action, a medium-fast flex rod allows for longer casts with lighter baits and lures. The weight of your lure and line can bend a medium-flex rod more deeply during the back cast, resulting in longer casts. If you're slinging live shrimp, go with a medium-fast rod. You'll also get a little more distance and softer landing when casting light, plastic-shrimp lures and small jerkbaits at spooky gators in skinny water.

Casting Gear

The feel of a favorite plug rod and reel is like a baseball glove you broke in yourself and have used for several seasons. There's also a feeling of control. You can stop a cast on a dime or add pressure on a fighting fish with a touch. Finally, there's a sense of belong-

ing to a tradition. Plug rods and reels are time-honored tackle.

Plug Reels

Plug casting tackle dates back at least to the 19th century. Although contemporary baitcasting reels are made of space-age aluminum and may sport fancy features such as magnetic anti-backlash systems,

their design fundamentally remains one of beautiful simplicity. They're timeless, and will always play an important role in the inshore angler's quiver.

Saltwater casting reels are made of non-corrosive reel parts, including stainless steel bearings, aluminum or graphite frames, and durable synthetic drag washers. There are two basic designs: the tradi-

tional round casting reel and the low-profile style. Some anglers prefer the round reel due to increased line capacity, and for bait fishing with heavier line. But even the biggest trout can't spool you, so the comfort of the more lightweight and ergonomic low-profile reels is more appealing.

Plug reels are defined by their revolving spools. Some models have removable side plates allowing for easy spool changes. Some reels have a side button

Some anglers use plug tackle exclusively when working topwater plugs. Short-handled models accommodate wade fishing. Right, traditional round casting reels and sleek, ergonomic low-profile models are options.

that disengages the spool for casting; others a centered thumb bar. Prior to casting, the angler depresses a button that puts the reel in freespool. The angler loads the rod with the weight of the lure and allows it to spring forward while applying the gentlest pressure to the spool. The pressure keeps the spool from overrunning, or spinning faster than the line can leave the reel. Overruns, or more commonly backlashes, are the result of too little pressure. Short, wild, splashy casts are the consequence of too much pressure. Most contemporary plug reels have adjustable centrifugal or magnetic brake systems that when set properly help prevent backlashes. But magnets are no substitute for a deft touch.

Magnetic breaks help avoid over-runs or "backlashes" when casting into a strong wind. A deft touch helps as well.

The angler must control the spool's rate of revolution with the thumb.

Many veteran trout anglers around the country use plug tackle exclusively. In Texas and the Central Gulf states, use of plug tackle is almost matter of piety. This preference is somewhat cultural, but plug tackle offers a number of distinct advantages. You can stop the revolving spool with thumb pressure instantly, allowing for pinpoint casts at potholes, docks or shorelines. With a heavy enough lure, good plug tackle in the right hands will out-distance spinning tackle. Drags are generally stronger, plus you can set the drag instantaneously by simply applying pressure with your thumb.

GUIDE'S PICK PLUG
Captain George Gozdz, Jensen Beach, FL

Rod
• 7-foot Fenwick Techna AVC70MHS Moderate Fast action

Reel
• Abu Garcia Revo Inshore

Line
• 30-pound Stren Superbraid

Leader
• 20-pound fluorocarbon

Plug reels come with a range of line retrieve ratios. Some have very high retrieve ratios, as many as seven turns of the spool to one turn of the reel handle. The ability to wind in slack quickly is important in situations where you're drifting down on your baits quickly, due to the wind or tide. If you're crawling jerkbaits and jigs through grass, you may want a reel with a 4.5: 1 or 5:1 ratio. These "low gear" reels also apply more torque on big fish. Choose a reel with a 5.7:1, 6.2:1 or even 7:1 gear ratio for working spoons, topwater plugs and spinners. There are a few multi-speed reels on the market.

Plug tackle does have a few disadvantages, most of which can be overcome with practice and proper selection of rod, reel and line. Casting into a strong wind can be difficult without backlashing. Finesse casts with light lures and baits are much harder, too, compared to appropriate spinning tackle. But with practice, finesse casts with light lures are achievable with plug tackle.

Plug Rods

Plug rods are the only type of rod with guides that ride on top of the rod. The reel faces up, so it follows that the guides do as well. They come in a wide variety of actions, and action should be matched to application. Most contemporary rods are made of sensitive graphite.

Long-handled rods are great for search casting, as they allow for two-hand casting and maximum distance. They can heave a topwater plug a long way, which allows you to cover a pile of water. For making long casts with lures weighing from 1/4 to 3/4 ounces, choose a 7-foot casting rod rated for 10- to 20-pound line. Shorter-handled rods are best for wading, because the short handle isn't as likely to splash the water or catch on wet, sagging shirt sleeves. Several manufacturers make plug rods designed specifically for wade fishing. These generally are short-handled rods that are at least 7 feet. Length is important since you're down in the water and already at elevation and leverage disadvantages. But some plug rods

Many experts maintain that you can keep more control of fish around the boat with plug tackle, because of the "thumb drag." Plug rod handles come in a variety of lengths and with various grips.

Rod handles come in different lengths and shapes. Short handles are for wading; longer handles leverage casting distance. Shape is important, too.

are short-handled and short in length. These rods are best for pitching under overhanging structure such as docks and mangroves. The short rod helps keep the cast low and on target.

Flex is another important consideration. Many topwater aficionados prefer a rod with a softer tip or medium-flex action which allows them to impart more subtle action on lures such as walking plugs. A softer tip also offers an angler a little built-in forgiveness when fishing on top. The worst thing you can do when a trout strikes a topwater plug is yank back on the fish immediately. If the fish is to be hooked the fish will hook itself. Jerking on the plug will either pull it away or pull the hooks out of the fish's soft mouth. But, it's hard to resist the temptation when a trout smacks that hardware. The softer tip may make the difference between a fish and a swing and a miss. A

softer tip also allows you to use lighter lures.

You should have one stiff, fast-flex plug rod in your quiver. You can still walk the dog with a stiff rod, and enjoy a few of the advantages of stiffness. In places, seagrass thickets and oyster reefs force you to fish with weedless lures, often Texas-rigged or "Tex-posed" plastic jerkbaits that require a strong hookset.

Stiff casting rods are hard to beat in terms of hook-setting power, particularly when fishing with Texas-rigged lures, suspending plugs or lures that employ large saltwater hooks or bait hooks. An angler first detects the strike, reels in the slack line, places the thumb on the spool and sets the hook firmly. This type of hookset, performed with a stout casting rod, usually results in a solid hookup. The stiff rod also helps you impart action on subsurface lures more directly.

Fly Gear

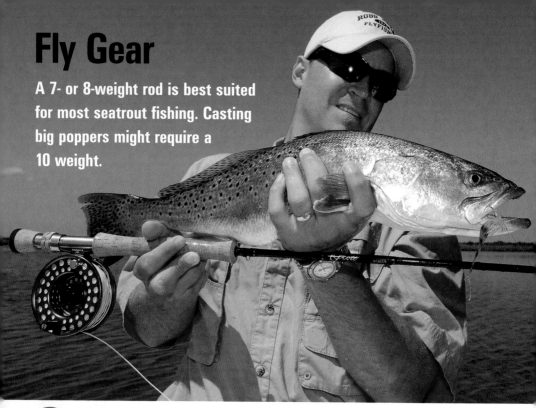

A 7- or 8-weight rod is best suited for most seatrout fishing. Casting big poppers might require a 10 weight.

Saltwater fly fishing did not take off until the 20th century, and it was largely an American phenomenon. Today, more and more anglers take on the challenges of saltwater fly fishing, and are learning that the art has its advantages.

Fly Rods

Fly fishing is an ancient art. The earli-est reference dates back to about the 4th century AD, when a poet named Aelian wrote of Macedonians catching trout on artificial flies and described how each fly was dressed. The rod they used was only 6 feet long and the line the same length, so that the method used was probably dapping the bait on the surface. We've come a long way in 17 centuries. A good caster with a modern graphite fly rod can hit a pie plate with a bulky fly more than 100 feet away.

When fishing for trout, many experts reserve the fly rod for highly technical situations, mainly sight fishing for gator trout in skinny water. Because the weight of the fly line loads the rod, not the weight of the fly, fly fishing allows you to make an almost silent presentation with a nearly weightless and highly imitative pattern. But fishing with popping bugs is an incredibly exciting way to get your topwater fix. And a variety of sinking lines makes prospecting with streamers more productive than ever.

Most saltwater fly rods are between eight feet, six inches and 10 feet long.

GUIDE'S PICK FLY
Captain John Meskauskas, Stuart, FL

Rod
· Loomis 7-weight GLX Crosscurrent

Reel
· Tibor Freestone

Line
· Clear intermediate-sink line

Leader
· 8- to 9-foot leader tapering to 20-pound fluorocarbon

The shorter sticks are either bluewater rods designed more to fight than cast or rods designed with the short game and overhanging cover in mind. Rods longer than 9 feet are made for wading. Double-handed rods that evolved from Spey fishing have also achieved some popularity. These rods may be 11 to 15 feet.

Fly rods are assigned a number that relates to line weight. The spectrum is amazing. A 0-weight rod is used in the tiniest fresh-water streams. A 15-weight "fighting stick" is the tool for sailfish, tuna and other pelagic giants. Six- through 10-weight rods are most commonly used in seatrout fishing, and most rods have a medium-fast or fast action. But the rod

Short rods are good for shorelines and dock work. Nine-footers are for distance casting.

number and line weight may not be an exact match. Most fast-action and some medium-action fly rods cast better when "over-lined" by one line weight. When learning to fly cast or teaching someone, you can help them feel what you mean by the "loading" the rod by overlining one or two numbers.

Six- and 7-weight rods are great for schoolie fish and for the calmest, most nerve-wracking sight-fishing scenarios. Eight- and 9-weight rods are much more versatile. The medium-fast action 8 or 9 weight is capable of making very delicate presentations. Medium-fast rods also better throw big, open loops when fishing with sinking lines, which prevents tangles and slappy, sloppy presentations.

Even big trout may not run far enough to take up all the slack fly line, so wind it up. Getting the fish "on the reel" is important for control.

Fast-action rods of the same weight can punch a small or medium-size fly through the wind, including poppers. And they can drag heavy trout out of seagrass. The 10-weight is reserved for large streamers and poppers, and/or for gator trout.

Fly Reels

Early fly reels didn't do much more than let line out and wind it in. The angler applied drag by cupping the spool. Anglers still use their hands to apply pressure, but modern reels sport adjustable disc drags. Some even have anti-reverse drags. Reels

Whether toying with schoolie trout or targeting gators, fly fishing ramps up the fun and challenge factors.

Most fly reels can be adjusted to right or left-hand retrieve, and offer interchangeable spools.

nowadays are made from light-weight aluminum, and many have quick-release spools for changing lines. Some also boast larger spools, or "arbors." With the exception of a few specialized multiplying models for big game, all fly reels have a 1:1 gear ratio, and while large-arbor reels weigh a little more, they have an advantage in how quickly they pick up line. Because the revolution distance is greater a large-arbor reel picks up more line per

turn than a reel with a standard arbor.

Large-arbor reels can feel a bit unwieldy on 7- and 8-weight rods. For most trout fishing, a fly reel doesn't need to hold more than 100 yards of 20-pound backing, and you can easily pack that much line and more on if you use 20-pound braided line on a standard-size reel. All fly reels are marked for a specific line weight or for a narrow range of line weights. If you intend to overload your rod, you need to purchase one size larger reel, or cut down on the amount of backing so that the fly line doesn't bind the reel.

For lefties, a left-handed retrieve makes more sense for line recovery, and vice versa for righties. The downside is you risk losing a fish while switching the rod over to the other hand.

Stripping basket, or Line Tamer, right, are superb line-management tools. Keep fly line clean and slick so it leaps through the guides.

Monofilament and braided lines have their respective applications. Some prefer mono for topwater fishing.

Lines

Some lines are better suited for specific types of trout fishing. The contemporary cornucopia of monofilament, fluorocarbon, hybrid, fused and braided lines each have distinct advantages and disadvantages. Many professional bass anglers keep rods rigged and ready at their feet spooled with various types of line. Seatrout anglers should take a cue from them.

Monofilament

Clear monofilament fishing lines began dominating the market in the early 1960s, after DuPont introduced Stren, a thinner monofilament line that could be used on a variety of reels, including newly introduced spinning and spincasting tackle. From freshwater to bluewater, monofilament remains the least expensive and most commonly used line. Manufacturers melt and mix nylon, then feed the molten material through holes of different diameter, depending upon the desired pound test. Color can be added for the sake of visibility or camouflauge.

Mono is stretchy, and its flexibility is part of its strength. Stretch somewhat forgives slow reflexes, wrapped rod tips or drags set too tight. But it reduces the power of the hookset and your ability to lift a heavy fish. Stretch also reduces sensitivity, and mono also has "memory." It takes the shape of the spool, which can lead to tangles, backlashes, twist and reduced casting distance.

The two trout fishing applications in which mono excels over other types of line are topwater plug/fly fishing and live baiting. Most topwater plugs have treble hooks, and monofilament, since it floats, is less inclined to tangle in the

hooks than fluorocarbon or braid. That buoyancy also helps you impart better action on topwater plugs, popping bugs, deerhair sliders and other flies. Thus, monofilament makes better leader material for topwater applications. Most importantly, monofilament's stretchiness helps reduce the tension when a trout

Most spinning reels come with an extra spool. You can keep one loaded with braid and one with monofilament.

strikes a topwater. It gives a little, which helps with topwater hookups.

Hybrid Lines

Recent innovations in "hybrid" lines include nylon copolymer-resin monofilaments and nylon/fluorocarbon combinations. Some of these pricy combinations are even stretchier than mono, which improves strength, casting ease and accuracy. Some combinations offer improved abrasion resistance.

Fluorocarbon, an extruded polymer, falls under this category and because it comes the closest to the light refractive index of water it is the least visible. Fluorocarbon is very expensive and most often used for leader material only.

Fly Lines

Fly lines are basically made of woven synthetic strands coated with several thin layers of plastic. The coating may have "air bubbles" or tungsten particles, and that quickly determines whether the line floats, sinks gradually or sinks. Older sinking lines actually had lead cores, but modern sinking lines use less toxic, space-age materials.

Most floating fly lines have a larger diameter and weight toward the head, hence the term "weight forward." The denser head helps load the rod and pulls

Slow-sinking lines and quick-sinking lines allow fly anglers to work the water column.

the lighter, thinner running (shooting) line through the rod guides when you cast. Slow- and intermediate-sink lines are weight-forward just like floaters. These lines are best for working deeper flats, beaches, shoals and shallow swift-moving water. Specialty sinking lines may have shooting heads attached to a running line with a splice. Shooting heads cast like a rocket and are great for making long prospecting casts through deep, fast channels and canals, and when surf fishing in heavy surf. The sinking line helps with distance and keeps the waves from buffeting the line and fly. Generally, the running line is much thinner and floats, so a bend develops in the line that makes the fly move more vertically. Regular, fully tapered, one-piece sinking lines are best when you want to dredge the bottom.

Braided Lines

In 1939, DuPont began marketing nylon monofilament fishing lines; however, braided Dacron lines remained the most used and popular fishing line for the next two decades. These lines were abrasion-resistant, basically stretch-free, and thus, sensitive. Many anglers have re-embraced these qualities in a fishing line, and now choose modern braided line for most inshore applications.

Braided lines are made by fusing or "braiding" gelspun polyethylene fibers. The main advantage is the strength it offers relative to diameter. Twenty-pound-test Spiderwire braid, for example, has the same diameter as 6-pound mono. It is also much more abrasion resistant than mono, a distinct advantage when fishing around oyster reefs and docks.

The most important advantage that braid affords trout anglers is hyper-sensitivity. It is very fine, limp and does not stretch. Especially in the winter, trout strikes often feel like grass pulling on your lure, but

Braided lines are worth the occasional "braid booger." If you manage your line correctly, you can reduce the occurrences.

even the subtlest takes are transmitted through braid.

The second most important advantage is casting distance. Small diameter and lack of memory and friction allow for much longer casts with much lighter lures. Braids come in a variety of colors, from neutral green or gray to high-viz yellow.

Some anglers try braided lines and go right back to monofilament or hybrid lines,

mainly because of braid's propensity to tangle. Dreaded "braid boogers" are usually very difficult to untangle, especially if the tangle has gotten wet. Depending on how deep the tangle is on your reel, you may end up cutting off $5 to $20 worth of line in one fell swoop. The stuff is expensive, and the first step in preventing frustrating tangles is spooling the line with proper tension and amount of line. Whenever possible, spin braid onto the spool with a machine. By closing the bail before the lure or bait lands, and by monitoring your reel for loops, you can largely avoid these dreaded knots.

Special attention must be paid when tying knots with braid, especially when joining braid to a different material. The braided line is often five or ten times smaller in diameter, so it's a good idea to double a short section of the braid before tying on your leader. Braid can also cut through monofilament and fluoro-

When using braid, make sure the line comes back on the spool evenly or "braid boogers," below, are the consequence.

carbon, or slip through it. Two of the best joining knots are the Albright and the double uni-knot. It's a good idea to make eight or nine wraps (to the four or five on the mono/fluoro side) when tying the braid side of the double uni-knot.

Braided lines should come with a Surgeon General's warning. The stuff is sharp and minutely serrated. It would make an excellent garrote. It often makes painful little cuts like paper cuts. It's also hard to break off when you get hung up, and a lot of rods have been broken by high-sticking with braid. Finally, when fishing with braid, you must remember to carry sharp scissors to cut the stuff. SB

Terminal Tackle

Most seatrout fishing involves fairly light leaders and terminal tackle. But a diverse array of terminal tackle is used in different applications. A fly caster may choose a No. 4 shrimp pattern when sight casting to spooky gators in shallow water. When prospecting, a plug caster may rig a 7-inch jerkbait Texas style, with a 5/0 or 6/0 "worm" hook. Different knots help ensure strong line/leader connections, or facilitate improved lure action.

A 12- to 36-inch piece of 12- to 20-pound fluorocarbon suffices for trout leader. Two- to 3-foot leaders are needed in very clear water.

Leaders

The first piece of terminal tackle is the leader, the segment of line attached directly to the hook. Leaders heavier than 20-pound test aren't needed for trout unless fishing in an area where rough-lipped species such as snook or stripers occur. This piece of leader may also be called a shock tippet. Generally 12- to 15-pound fluoro-carbon will suffice for subsurface presentations. Mono is not as invisible or as abrasion resistant, but it floats so it's better for surface lures and flies. When fishing with monofilament line, many trout anglers simply tie the lure directly to the line, side-stepping the leader altogether.

You can get away with a very short leader in the off-color water such as the waters of the Louisiana bayous. But as much as three feet may be necessary on

It's always a good idea to mash down your barbs. You get better penetration and it's much easier to get a fish off the hook without harming it or yourself.

Trout look like the bottoms they swim over, which are usually covered in grass or oysters. Weedless lures are often necessary.

the air-clear flats of the Indian River Lagoon or Lower Laguna Madre.

In most applications, the shock tippet is attached directly to the main line or fly leader with a knot such as the Albright special, blood knot, or double uni-knot. Rigging soft-plastic jerkbaits or natural baits behind a sliding sinker rig is also effective. Then, a small swivel makes the connection between leader and main line, to keep the sinker a certain minimum distance above the offering. When fishing

with spoons, snap swivels are a good idea because they reduce line twist.

Fly leaders and shock tippets are a different business altogether. You can't or at least wouldn't want to tie a fly directly to the fly line. And you want the leader to unfurl evenly, without hinging and without the "dying quail" effect that's a symptom of a too-long light section. First, attach a butt section of monofilament that is about the same diameter as the fly line and is about 60 percent of the total leader length. Forty-pound test is pretty universal. Then attach a tapered leader of your own with each section shorter than the previous section.

Commercially made, tapered leaders are generally knotless, and are better in weedy situations. If you build your own leaders, use the slimmest knots possible, trim them closely, and make each segment slightly longer than the next. Leader lengths will range from 6 to 12 feet when fishing floating or intermediate-sink lines in relatively clear water. In most circumstances, you can get away with a 3- to 6-foot piece of light fluorocarbon when fishing full sinking lines. It's very hard to turn over a long leader with a sinking line, and frankly, trout down deep are rarely line shy.

> For invisibility and safety, fluorocarbon leaders are essential when fishing with braided line. When landing a struggling fish, braided line can slice like a sharp paper edge.

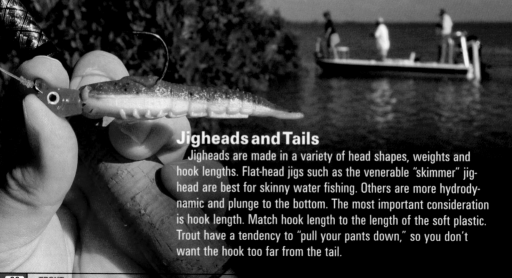

Jigheads and Tails

Jigheads are made in a variety of head shapes, weights and hook lengths. Flat-head jigs such as the venerable "skimmer" jighead are best for skinny water fishing. Others are more hydrodynamic and plunge to the bottom. The most important consideration is hook length. Match hook length to the length of the soft plastic. Trout have a tendency to "pull your pants down," so you don't want the hook too far from the tail.

Bait Hooks

Thankfully, circle hooks are increasingly popular among bait fishermen. Circle hooks rarely gut hook a fish. Usually, they wind up in the corner of the jaw where they are easy to remove. It's also rare to miss a fish when using a circle hook, because as long as you resist the temptation to strike suddenly the hook will set itself in the corner of the jaw. Hook size is relative to bait size. Use a No. 1 circle hook for small live shrimp or small baitfish such as mud minnows. A 5/0 or larger hook is appropriate for large mullet or cutbaits. Kahle hooks or worm hooks are also great for rigging shrimp weedless.

Jerkbait Hooks

Seatrout tactics and freshwater tactics often converge, most often when soft-plastic baits are employed. When Texas-rigging baits, worm hooks should also be used, but make sure you buy the anodized saltwater variety. Small jerkbaits and artificial shrimp lures may require a hook as small as 3/0. Lengthy jerkbaits require as large as a 6/0 hook. A wide gap is important. Weighted worm hooks and hooks with head screws to hold the jerkbait are handy alternatives.

Fly Hooks

Most fly tying for saltwater fishing is done on steel or thin, wire J-hooks. A few conservation-minded anglers use circle hooks, but it is hard to resist the temptation of setting the hook. Weedless bendback patterns can be tied upside down on Kahle hooks, or more commonly on J-hooks bent slightly back behind the eye. Hooks for popping bugs are uniquely shaped and usually very sharp wire hooks.

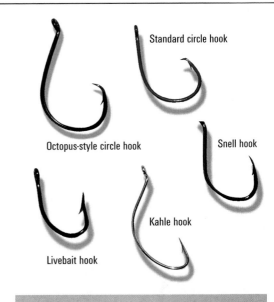

Standard circle hook

Octopus-style circle hook

Snell hook

Kahle hook

Livebait hook

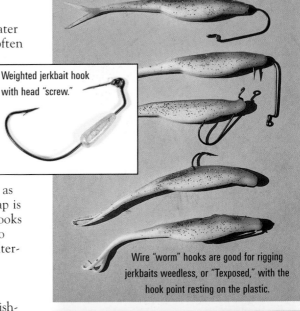

Weighted jerkbait hook with head "screw."

Wire "worm" hooks are good for rigging jerkbaits weedless, or "Texposed," with the hook point resting on the plastic.

Most hooks for streamer flies are types of J-hooks.

Landing Gear

Tackle needs don't end with the hook on the end of the line. Let's look at some of the devices which help you land a fish and perhaps release it without hurting the fish or yourself. Landing nets, fish-holding grippers, gloves, towels and hook removers are important to keep onboard or on your person.

trol. Unless you're taking the fish home for dinner, you might leave the netted fish in the water and remove the hook there. When you remove a fish from the water, it experiences several times the amount of gravity that it does under water. Increased weight from gravity can damage organs, plus, they obviously can't breathe above water. If sharks, barracudas or porpoises are present, a net helps you keep the fish under control until you can release it into safer waters.

Landing nets come in a number of shapes and sizes. Make sure the net is wide enough to land as big a trout as you can expect to catch. Trout are fragile fish. They lack the scale armor of their cousins, the redfish, and a coat of slime and delicate skin is all that protects them from laceration and infection. Net mesh is usually nylon, but rubber-mesh nets are much more fish-friendly. Rubber is soft, and doesn't remove the essential coating of slime, which protects the fish against disease. Hooks are also removed from rubber nets far more easily. The tighter the mesh, the better, from the standpoint of minimizing damage to fish fins. Telescopic handles allow you to reach out to your catch and still stow conveniently. Netting the fish away from the boat prevents the fish from hurting itself while thrashing boatside.

When using a landing net, try to net the fish head first or get the net completely under the fish and lift.

Trout commonly get off right at the boat. The fish points its head right at you, and shakes it violently. Nets and grippers reduce the number of fish lost boatside.

Landing Nets

The landing net has a time-honored position on a seatrout angler's boat. Today, some authorities caution that it's best not to net fish, but a net helps you get a fish under con-

A net can minimize how much you handle the fish. Slime is the first line of defense for a trout's immune system, so handle a big girl like this fish with care.

If you want to get a picture with a trophy-class fish, wet your hands or better yet, use a wet towel and support the fish with your hand under its abdomen.

A wet towel will remove less slime than a dry one.

Above, a de-hooker is the gentlest way to remove a hook from deep in a trout's throat. Trigger action backs the point out. Lawsticks, below, are important if you want to keep fish. Mind those limits.

Hanging a fish by the gills, lips or jaw can do irreparable damage to feeding and breathing organs, and dislocate vertebrae.

Gloves

Wearing gloves is in the fish's best interests as well as your own. Wet gloves remove less fish slime, while they protect the angler from hook points, fin pokes and a number of nasty marine diseases such as flesh-eating bacteria. Limbs and even lives have been lost to *Vibrio vulnificus*, a bacteria that likes back bays. Guides on Florida's St. Lucie River complained of staph infections during 2005, when the U.S. Army Corps of Engineers pumped 300 billion gallons of nutrient-laden, algae-bloom covered runoff into North America's most biologically diverse estuary.

Hook Removers

The most basic hook remover has a U-shaped end with a narrow gap. Some have a trigger and pulley system. For deeply hooked fish, slide the end down the line, over the hook and then back it out. Sometimes you just have to break out the pliers, but hook removers provide a lot of torque in tight places. They're also a lot easier on the fish. Always avoid touching the gills. Finally, hooks are much easier to remove if you mash down the barb or barbs with pliers. Barbs aren't needed if you keep a tight line.

Rulers

If you're fishing a tournament, or plan to take home a fish, it's imperative that you know and conform to the size- and bag-limit regulations. The *Florida Sportsman Communications Network* offers lawsticks for most states, with size limits of the most popular gamefish species printed on them. There are also adhesive "bumper sticker" style rulers to stick on the deck of a boat. **SB**

Control the Head; Support the Body

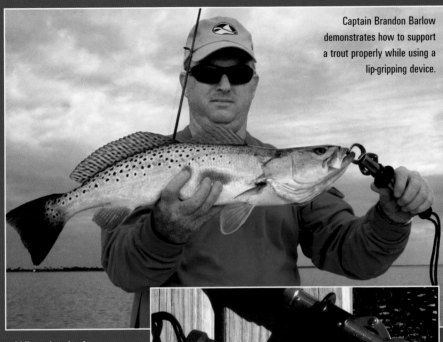

Captain Brandon Barlow demonstrates how to support a trout properly while using a lip-gripping device.

When hooked, trout are notorious headshakers. Often they keep right on shaking while you try to get the hook out. By controlling a fish's head, you help protect the fish and yourself.

You can lip a trout like a bass, but you risk hooking yourself if you do. And those canine teeth in there can penetrate deeply. Metal or plastic grippers put some distance between hook, teeth and hand. Simply place the prongs around the tip of the fish's lower jawbone and release the trigger. The weight of the fish causes the prongs to shut even tighter, and a locking mechanism keeps prongs in the tightest position. Some models even have shock absorbers.

Some grippers are also scales, but bear in mind that studies indicate you can kill a fish by hanging it vertically out of the water from its jaws. One way to size up your fish accurately is to place the fish in a net and hook the grippers to the rim of the net. Weigh the fish in the net and then release it. Then weigh the net and subtract its weight from the first measurement. SB

CHAPTER 5

Trout Boats

T here's no one vessel ideally suited to catch spotted seatrout in all situations. Fortunately, many types of boats and propulsion can put you on trout.

Most trout fishing isn't very technical. It typically involves drifting 3- to 4-foot-deep flats in coastal bays or bayous. You rarely need a highly specialized boat. Odds are, a bay boat is exactly what you need. Many sport a long list of fishing accessories.

If you're really into targeting gator trout in very skinny water, contemporary technical poling skiffs are the form-and-function epitome of stealth.

The tunnel skiff is a Texas classic. These boats are used primarily to carry a number of anglers across very shallow water to productive wading areas.

A number of classic flat-bottom skiffs, both fiberglass and aluminum, have been mainstay inshore vessels for nearly half a century.

Stealthy kayaks and canoes allow you to get close to wary gators. Canoes glide shallow, are quiet, and allow you to fish with a buddy.

Even the simplest vessels get you into trout. In some places, kayaks and canoes are best for approaching big fish.

See DVD for more on picking the right boat.

These anglers converted a venerable Gheenoe into a flats fishing machine. Above, if you live on the water, keeping the boat on a lift reduces maintenance.

The Fleet

The most important factors in buying a boat are choosing one that suits the waters and accommodates your needs.

Some anglers prefer to buy a brand new boat replete with options. Do-it-yourselfers may invest in a classic hull and build a customized dream boat. For them, pride of ownership is almost as important as catching fish. Even canoes and kayaks can be engineered with a variety of sophisticated fishing equipment, including livewells and fishfinder/chartplotter machines. Part of the fun is tricking out your ride.

Bay Boats

Modern bay boats—slightly larger, higher-sided inshore boats—are popular and comfortable inshore vessels. Bay boats range from 19 to 24 feet and may weigh up to 2,500 pounds. A wide beam—up to 96 inches—creates enough displacement that these relatively large boats float in 10

resins and hand-laid fiberglass. Some integrate flotation compartments to ensure an unsinkable hull. High-tech stringer systems tie into the hull, transom and deck to work as one unit so

to 15 inches. Some can handle up to a 300-horsepower engine, which obviously can get you on the fish, fast.

In terms of hull integrity and layout, these boats are engineering marvels. Premium bay boats are built with special

Bay boat with spacious foredecks allows two anglers to fish safely and comfortably from the bow. Boats with higher gunnels and deeper cockpit, such as this Century model, are safer for kids.

there's less torque. Hull separation is rarely a problem these days. Bay boats are roomier and more comfortable than traditional johnboats or small skiffs. Most come with one or two livewells, and an additional release well. Anglers can rest their knees against the gunnels and the wider boats are stable, so you don't have to spend the day on your toes balancing in a chop. They fish more anglers and take on chop better than flats skiffs.

Bay boats also are family friendly. You trade 360-degree fishability for shade, but they're wide enough for a T-top or Bimini top. Some offer a leaning post and forward padded seating. If there's a downside to these utility vessels, it's that they burn a little more fuel than smaller boats. Four-stroke outboards and some 2-strokes offer improved fuel efficiency and larger fuel cells allow for incredible range, up to 300 miles in some boats.

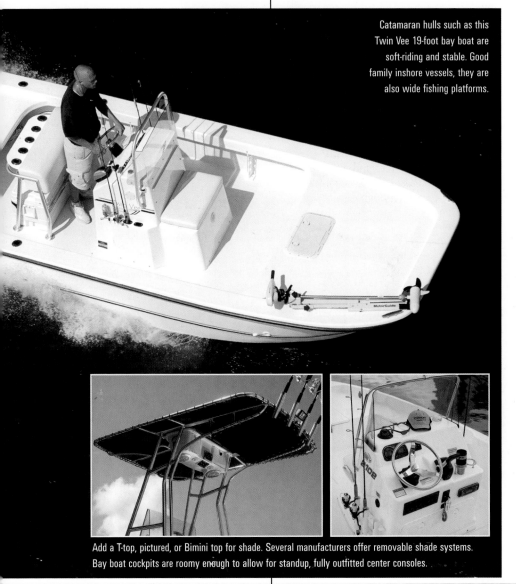

Catamaran hulls such as this Twin Vee 19-foot bay boat are soft-riding and stable. Good family inshore vessels, they are also wide fishing platforms.

Add a T-top, pictured, or Bimini top for shade. Several manufacturers offer removable shade systems. Bay boat cockpits are roomy enough to allow for standup, fully outfitted center consoles.

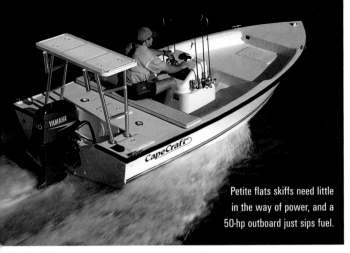

Petite flats skiffs need little in the way of power, and a 50-hp outboard just sips fuel.

They're basically low-sided bay boats.

Poling skiffs can weigh as little as 500 pounds and draw from 5 to 10 inches. The shallowest draft poling skiffs are called technical poling skiffs. Designed more with bonefishing and redfishing in mind, technical poling skiffs are also ideal for pursuing an equally if not more diffi-

Poling Skiffs

Poling skiffs are the vessels most commonly used to fish the shallow flats. These boats generally range between 15 and 19 feet, but a few 20-foot "crossover skiffs" are on the market. You can pole a crossover skiff, but it isn't a lot of fun.

cult quarry—gator trout laid up in shin-deep water.

Trout can feel pressure waves sent out from the bow and can feel and hear the sound of waves lapping at the hull from far away. Much work has gone into reducing the pressure wave and hull slap on

A technical poling skiff may be best if your trout waters are especially shallow

Most big trout landed on fly are caught by teams sight fishing in poling skiffs.

technical poling skiffs, and these boats almost pole silently. Technical skiffs are lightweight, one-piece hulls often made of Kevlar. Max horsepower on these fighter jets of the flats range from 25 to 70 hp.

The tradeoff with poling skiffs, especially with technical poling skiffs, is a comfortable ride. In glassy conditions these boats handle like racing boats, but chop and boat wakes turn an exhilarating ride into a rough, wet one. In very few places does trout fishing require you to float in less than 6 inches. A larger poling skiff, a boat in the 17- to 19-foot range, handles rough water much better, accommodates at least one more angler and heaps more gear, and floats in less than 10 inches. Larger skiffs may weigh up to 1,500 pounds, have more than one livewell and a larger 30- to 50-gallon fuel cell. Maximum hp ratings range from 90 to 200.

r provide sight-fishing opportunities.

Big Trout Boats

Day after day, in larger coastal rivers and sounds, countless seatrout hit the iceboxes of 18- to 24-foot vee-hull center consoles and cabin cruisers. These boats are rarely configured or powered for silent operation in the shallows, but that's no matter. Some of the best seatrout action takes place in deep

Large vessels catch plenty of trout where water depths allow. Good fun for the whole family.

holes, particularly in cooler months. On brackish rivers along the Gulf of Mexico and lower Atlantic coasts, it's common to see families fishing aboard boats big enough to tackle the open ocean. Indeed, on calm summer days, many of these "trout boats" will be found 20 miles offshore on the mackerel or snapper grounds. Careful skippers have no trouble manuevering these boats to drift lower bay grassflats.

Some decided advantages over the shallow-water fleet include full-height gunnels, weather protection, and space for an array of gear. A small cabin or pilot house can be a real comfort on freezing winter mornings. Full canvas enclosures, attached to a Bimini or hardtop, are also popular options. SB

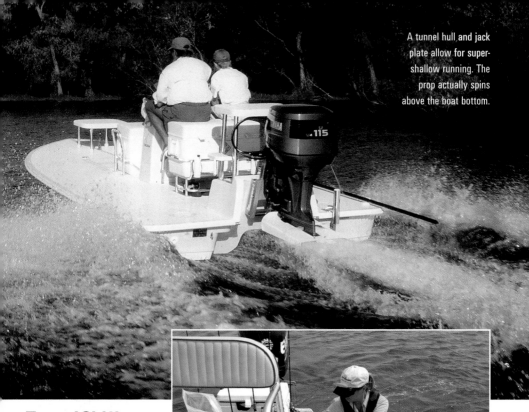

A tunnel hull and jack plate allow for super-shallow running. The prop actually spins above the boat bottom.

Tunnel Skiffs

Tunnel skiffs are a Texas invention and they make great inshore fishing vessels. In fact, in the 1960s, Texans invented the first of these "scooter" boats for fishing the state's shallow bays. Falcon Boat founders Willis Hudson and Rex Hudson of Shallow Sport Boats are credited with being among the first to experiment with fiberglass hulls and for refining the design. In the '80s, the family founded Shallow Sport Boats, which remains one of the most successful tunnel skiff manufacturing companies. Tunnel boats dominate the Texas market, are often used along the Central Gulf Coast, and are becoming increasingly popular in the waters of Florida, Georgia and the Carolinas.

One or, more recently, two tunnels run

Most Texas tunnel skiffs have very low gunnels so that waders can climb in and out easily.

down through the center of the hull. The boat gets on plane like a hydroplane hull, but feels almost like a catamaran. They don't have sponsons per se, but the lateral hulls behave somewhat like sponsons, lending the boat stability as well as a quick liftoff.

The boats are famous for taking chop well. Without a keel, they feel like they float over waves. An upturned bow keeps the spray down. Even tunnel skiffs on the larger end of the inshore spectrum, boats in the 24-foot range, run in very shallow water. A tunnel running down the center of the hull makes it so that the prop need not be deeper than the hull. In fact, a jack plate is used to keep the motor well above the hull bottom. The width of the boat and lack of hull curve, along with the jack plate, allow tunnel skiffs to run in only a few inches of water. But keep in mind that any boat can damage a grassflat.

Fishability is an interesting concept in the context of Texas inshore fishing and tunnel skiffs. Wading is the way tradition-al Texas inshore fishing is done, and tunnel skiffs have very low gunnels to make it easy for waders to get in and out of the boat. Most have flush decks. You can also easily fish from the boat, and landing and releasing a fish doesn't require much more than taking a knee.

Hull slap is one of the few drawbacks to tunnel skiffs. Waves pound the inside of the tunnel, making it more difficult to stalk fish in a chop.

Flat-bottom **Boats**

Many a budget-limited seatrout angler has turned a flat-bottom fiberglass skiff or aluminum john-boat into a custom inshore fishing machine. Durable aluminum boats are especially desirable if you fish around shallow oyster reefs.

Flat-bottom boats are easy to customize. You can trick one out with a poling platform, fishfinder, multiple baitwells, large cooler and even go so far as adding a tower if the hull is wide and stable enough.

A custom-rigged johnboat became one angler's dreamboat.

These boats are light, stable and float in very shallow water. The downside is that they pound you in choppy conditions. Flat-bottom boats don't track as well when poled compared to a skiff with some keel, but they certainly pole well enough. If you plan on spending a lot of time drift fishing for a limit of trout or baitfishing in back-country creeks, a flat-bottom skiff may be all that you need.

If you stalk skinny water only part of the time, and fish or duck hunt in areas where combustion engines aren't allowed, a canoe-skiff hybrid such as the Gheenoe is a great, inexpensive option. These are square-backed canoes that allow a small outboard to be removed easily. You can mount poling and casting platforms as well. SB

FL2491NA   Gheenoe

Several canoe-shaped mini-skiffs are on the market. They are inexpensive, run super shallow, and can be customized into superb fishing machines.

Cartoppers

If there's roadside access in the area you want to fish for seatrout, or if you like to get some exercise while fishing, a canoe or kayak is the way to go. Plus, you'll save heaps of money on gas.

Canoes and kayaks get you where power boats can't or aren't allowed to go. Solitude and less wary fish are the rewards.

Most kayaks run in the 50- to 70-pound range. Two anglers can easily lift one, and there are tools to help the solitary angler get the boat on and off the roof.

Canoes

Canoes are the most versatile paddle-powered craft, and they don't necessarily have to be paddle-powered. Special mounts are available that allow you to attach a small electric or combustion motor, generally 4 horsepower or less. You can even attach stabilizing outriggers that allow two anglers to stand and sight fish.

Most canoes for saltwater inshore applications are pretty long, wide and straight. The most expensive and lightest models are made of carbon-Kevlar composites, but aluminum or Duratex-finished boats are relatively inexpensive and last longer around oyster bars and limestone reefs. Most canoes used frequently in salt water live a tough life, so go with these materials if you fish in waters rife with submerged or emergent hazards.

Agile anglers can stand and fish in a canoe. Stabilizing outriggers make it safer.

This customized kayak bristles with rod holders, depth recorder, compass, anchor pulley system and light. It's a stealth attack machine.

Kayaks

The popularity of kayak fishing is exploding, and for good reason: Kayaks are deadly fishing machines. They run silent and shallow, shallower than just about any flats skiff on the market. Polyethylene materials allow some kayaks to float in two inches, unless the angler shops at Big & Tall.

The sit-on-top varieties are the most popular because you can get in and out of the boat more easily, and they afford the fisherman a little height advantage. And should it flip, the sealed hull won't fill with water, unlike sit-inside models.

Longer, 15- to 18-foot boats are faster— long, narrow boats are often referred to as touring kayaks. They're great for long-range camping trips, but are limited in terms of fishability. They have traded agility and stability for raw speed.

Most fishing kayaks are 9 to 14 feet, with 28- to 34-inch beams. Wider kayaks are more stable and hold more gear. But short, ultralight models are available that weigh as little as 30 pounds. Your average 13-foot sit-on-top weighs 50 to 70 pounds.

Kayaking is a great way to get some fun exercise. If you use a paddle, you'll get a good workout on arm, back, shoulder and stabilizer muscles. If you use foot pedals, your leg muscles get the burn. Pedal-powered boats leave hands free for fishing, but draw a little more water because of the penguin-like flippers under the boat.

Storage and accessibility are huge factors in choosing a kayak. Sealed hatches can keep things dry but some designs can be hard to access while sitting in the boat. Several boats are so roomy they allow fully rigged 9-foot fly rods to be stowed inside. SB

Pedal kayaks with lever-controlled rudders leave hands free for casting— and far more importantly, for fighting fish.

CHAPTER 6

Rigging Boats for Seatrout Fishing

A variety of boats are used to catch trout, including large vee-hulls, bay boats, flats skiffs, flat-bottom skiffs, johnboats, canoes and kayaks. You should choose a boat and customize it according to the style or styles of fishing you do most. Some options, including jack plates and trim tabs, can improve performance. On flats skiffs, as well as some bay boats and johnboats, poling platforms, casting platforms and towers give sight fishermen an edge. Carpet or pad products such as those made by SeaDek offer non-skid marine traction that make a boat quieter, reduce fatigue and make a boat less dangerous when the deck is covered in blood and slime. Even in small boats there are several options to create shade. And in the fishing department, livewells keep bait frisky and keepers fresh, while vertical rod holders keep rods handy and rod lockers keep them safe. Choosing the best options will lend considerably to fishing success.

Customizing your ride is addicting. You can add a variety of tools to increase your success. Buying or building the perfect inshore boat becomes a lifelong quest.

This flats skiff is fully rigged, with a Power-Pole (foreground), poling platform, pushpole, jack plate, trim tabs, livewells and electric trolling motor.

Trout Out Your Boat

Seatrout fishing takes place in such wildly different habitats that rigging a boat "right" is a subjective affair. Bait-fishing anglers may want additional baitwells and rod holders. Sight-fishing devotees need poling and casting platforms. Every boat needs an anchor, but different anchors work better in different types of bottom. Drift fishing is often far more productive with a sea anchor, also called a drogue or wind sock.

There's a whole suite of appliances for kayaks and canoes.

Electric motors

An electric trolling motor is just about indispensable for trout fishing. Most motors are bow-mounted, but stern-, trim-tab- and engine-mounted models are available. Forward-mounted electric motors are tough to beat for controlling the bow and working water methodically.

Anglers can opt for two types of electric motor controls: remote control and hand control. Hand-control units may be the most dependable, but remote control technology improves every year. It's liberating

Hands-free, wireless electric trolling motors make inshore fishing easier. The remote can be worn around your neck (inset), which keeps hands free for landing fish.

being able to control the bow from anywhere in the boat.

Today's electric trolling motors are quieter and more powerful than ever; but a motor is only as stealthy as it is operated. In order to operate an electric motor without spooking fish, you need to make sure the propeller is fully underwater so it can't splash or cavitate. Also, make sure that it's not mowing the grass or smacking into the bottom. You would not believe the noise a prop makes against grass blades underwater. Finally, the real key to catching fish is to operate the electric motor at low speed. Low speeds reduce hull slap and the sound of the propeller itself. By moving slowly and steadily, you avoid bumping fish. A constant hum underwater may not bother fish at all, but changes in speed may. You also allow everyone onboard to better manage their lines, stay tight to lures and avoid drag.

Shaft length is an important consideration. They generally range from 50 to 60 inches. Larger boats such as bay boats need the longer shaft and additional torque. Electric motors come in 12- , 24- and 36-volt models. Twelve-volt models will propel an aluminum johnboat or small skiff with 54 pounds of thrust. Twenty-four-volt electric motors work best on flats boats and flat-bottom fiberglass skiffs. They offer 70 to 82 pounds of thrust. Thirty-six-volt motors produce more than 100 pounds of thrust.

While handy, trolling motors are usually the most fickle machine on the boat. Keeping the battery or batteries charged prolongs their life. Unless you have an in-line cutoff switch, it's very important to unplug the electric motor when you get home, or the unit may still slowly drain

Large livewell gives large baits ample space to stay frisky. The drain pipe in the center keeps it from overflowing. Most bay boats offer standard or optional live- and release wells.

the battery. An onboard charger is most efficient, but a portable charger will work just fine. Try to keep connections free of corrosion and always carry spare fuses.

Livewells

At least one built-in livewell is standard issue on most inshore boats. But when fishing with crabs or shrimp, you can get away with a bait bucket or 5-gallon bucket and aerator. If your boat isn't equipped with a livewell or if you need a larger system for larger, friskier live baits such as pinfish or mullet, portable, re-circulating, battery-powered livewell systems are the way to go. Up to 10-gallon portable units will also fit in canoes and kayaks.

These days, thanks to the tournament redfishing craze, many flats and bay boats come with a large "release well." But release wells also make great baitwells, and you can use it to revive a big, tired fish before releasing it. And man, do they hold a lot of beer and ice.

Anchoring Devices

Every boat needs an anchor that is adequate to hold it in position in deeper water, strong current and wind, as well as sufficient line. The fluke-style Danforth anchor is far and away the most commonly used style of anchor. A 9-pound, 24-inch Danforth will hold most inshore boats.

So long as the wind or tide isn't too strong, mushroom-style anchors can be

You can pole from the deck, but a poling platform offers much more leverage and greater field of vision. A rod holder allows the poling angler to keep a rod handy. A pole clip provides a place to quietly stow the pushpole before making a cast.

From left, Sea-Cure (also in foreground), grapnel, and slip-ring Danforth-style anchors. Select according to boat size and bottom type. Top, rub rail protects the boat from the anchor chain. Make sure the anchor doesn't swing back and ding the bow.

used in small skiffs or canoes and kayaks. Mushroom anchors deploy easily and fairly quietly. Canoeists and kayakers favor 4-pronged, 1½- to 3-pound folding anchors. A slide goes down and locks the prongs into place. Folded up, they're compact and fit in any little cubby hole in the canoe or kayak.

Anglers often come upon schools of trout when drifting or working an area with the

Poling and Casting Platforms

Poling and casting platforms were designed to help sight-fishing teams see fish and fish signs better while poling clear, skinny flats. But whether poling, drifting or using an electric trolling motor, they offer tremendous visual advantages, especially in low light or high sun. Even with a high, bright sun, you can put the sun at your back and get above the glare. The extra height also adds to casting distance.

You'll find platforms on an array of inshore boats besides flats skiff, including bay boats, flat-bottom skiffs, and even large square-sterned canoes such as the venerable Gheenoe. Poling platforms average 3 to 4 feet high. They come in different sizes and widths, with the lower and smaller ones appropriate for technical poling skiffs and canoes.

A bow-mounted casting platform also gives the casting angler a much better field of vision. Platforms are usually anchored to the deck by a turnbuckle.

Rod holders can be attached to a poling platform, within easy reach of the poling angler in case a fish gets around to a four- to six-o'clock angle, or for trolling or trailing a live bait. The poling angler can quickly place the pole in a "snubber," a concave rubber clip on the top of the platform. Belt clips and clips that attach on the side of the platform are other options, as are bungee cords and rope. These devices also come into play when a pole is used to stake the boat out if you come upon a school or want to get out and wade.

Pushpoles

A pushpole is an indispensable tool for stalking gator trout in a skiff on a shallow flat. It's also handy to have aboard in case your electric motor goes on strike or runs out of juice.

Poling is quieter than running a trolling motor and the gentle splashes that you do make with the pole must sound like waves or jumping mullet because fish are rarely both-

ered by the sound. If the wind is light enough, poling also gives you greater control over the boat. The poling angler can adjust the bow angle for an optimal casting angle by turning the boat on its axis. A pole also can serve as an anchor for staking out.

Matching pole size to boat size and the depth of waters you fish is the most important consideration when investing in a pushpole. Poles range from 5-foot kayak-specific models to 24-foot models. Most skiff and bay boat owners opt for 18- to 20-foot poles.

Don't skimp on a cheap pole if you plan on using one for hours and hours on end. The more expensive models are made of graphite and run upward of $950, but a 20-foot model may weigh as little as 2.5 pounds. If you just want a pole as a backup source of propulsion and an anchor, fiberglass poles are much less expensive and more durable, but of course heavier. Some anglers simply go with a 12-foot piece of PVC pipe capped at both ends. Graphite/fiberglass hybrid pushpoles make a great compromise. You sacrifice a bit of stiffness with a two-piece model, but they obviously stow much more easily and even fit in some rod lockers and under-gunnel rod holders. SB

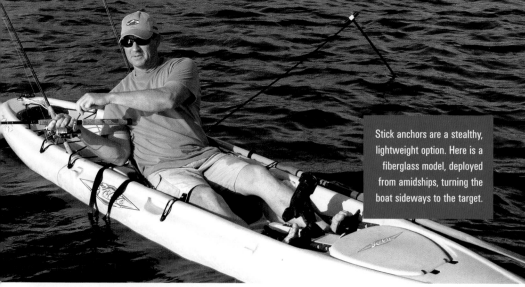

Stick anchors are a stealthy, lightweight option. Here is a fiberglass model, deployed from amidships, turning the boat sideways to the target.

Power-Pole is a stern-mounted graphite stick anchor operated remotely. Below, drogues, also called "sea anchors" and "drift socks," slow the vessel while drifting.

rod holders for storage. You tie off to the pin with floating lanyard, such as braided ⅜-inch dockline with 6-inch loops for tying off to your boat cleats or looping back through your stern trailer tie down. One is 24 inches for stern anchoring and one is 72 inches for bow anchoring. They run about $75.

The Cajun Anchor is also in this genre. This stainless steel spear anchor comes in 3- to 6-foot sizes to fit an array of vessels, from kayaks to large center-console bay boats. They run from $75 to $95.

The Power-Pole shallow water anchor is also a stick/spear style anchor, but this invention is attached to the stern. With the touch of a button, you activate the quiet hydraulic action by remote control and a 6- or 8-foot composite spike shoots into the bottom. Complete systems run from $1,300 to $1,500.

Sea Anchors

Sea anchors, sometimes called "drogues," or most commonly "drift socks," can be the difference between catching fish on a windy day and just going for a sail. They are chutes made of nylon or canvas deployed to slow your drift over a flat.

Deploy one sock from the stern, and the boat will drift bow-first and downwind. You can maneuver the bow with a bow-mounted electric trolling motor or cant it in either direction by turning the lowered

trolling motor. You want to stay in the school, and stick-style anchors deploy quickly and quietly in shallow water.

An example is the Stick It Anchor Pin. It is a 7-foot by 5/8-inch pole made of reinforced fiberglass. It comes with two C clips that can be mounted alongside your outboard left or right. This approach is best when working a shoreline parallel to the wind direction or when fishing an open flat by yourself.

When drift fishing an open flat with multiple anglers onboard, you can make the boat "crab" across the flat sideways if you deploy the sea anchor from amidships. You might keep two drift socks aboard, for high-wind situations. If you deploy one from the stern and one from the bow, the boat will drift sideways downwind. You can angle the boat by canting the outboard in one direction or the other.

Electronics

Thanks to the marvels of Global Positioning System (GPS) and sonar technologies, learning new seatrout fishing areas has never been easier. Many units come with both GPS and bottom-sounding capacities. Even canoeists and kayakers are reaping the benefits, with handheld GPS units or fix-mounted systems that have both capabilities.

An advanced digital chartplotter equipped with the proper chart card or built-in data can display all of the details you would look for in a traditional paper chart. Still, it's prudent to carry the correct paper chart as a backup. You can buy charts that your machine uploads for virtually any inshore area in the country. Fugawi introduced GPS/bottom sounder systems that allow you to run crisp satellite imagery from a Google Earth plug-in so you can view location imagery alongside the chart as you run.

Enter waypoint and the GPS will give you a bearing on the spot that you want to fish. Some units let you just click a cursor on the spot and off you go. A trail indicates where you've been, and marks

Sidescan sonar has recently become affordable. Though mostly used by blue-water anglers to "see" laterally, they may be useful for locating structure in deepwater trout fishing situations. Handheld radios, left, are portable options.

the way back home. Units also identify hazards such as wellheads and oyster bars. Tide and temperature readings are more bonuses on some units. You can find out exactly what the tide is doing by moving the cursor to a tide gauge icon on the map mode.

Fishfinder technology is especially important in finding deepwater trout haunts, such as scattered rocks, a deep slough through a flat, or deep holes in a marshy creek or river.

Finally, in the age of cellular telephones, it's vital to remember the benefits of marine VHF radios. Take both, and make sure the cell battery is charged, but keep in mind that you may not get a cellular signal in some wilderness areas. A VHF radio will at least keep you in contact with other VHF operators; range depends on power and antenna. With a marine radio, you can monitor the airwaves for fishing reports. Hand-held units are usually adequate inshore, but they lack the range of a fix-mount radio. SB

CHAPTER 7

Tides

In most places, the tide is the most important influence on when and where seatrout feed. Slack tides are usually the worst times to fish. Generally, the best bite occurs at the start of the flood or ebb. In areas such as Low Country marshes where the bottom is primarily silt, the fishing will almost certainly be best at the start of moving water because at that point the water is as clear as it will get. The tide is not yet running hard enough to stir up the sediment.

Water depth and tides influence water temperature as well. In the summer, fishing on an incoming tide close to an inlet or pass is a good idea, because the ocean water running into the estuary is likely cooler, invigorating their appetites. In winter, a shallow mud flat may fish better and better as the tide falls, because the mud is more able to soak up heat in shallow water. The warming coaxes shrimp and other forage out of dormancy, and spurs the metabolism of trout.

For safety's sake and for the sake of catching fish, the most important things to know as you plan a fishing trip are the times and ranges of the tides.

Intertidal oyster bars are major fish attractors. Trout will lie among the submerged shells or right on the edge.

Heavenly Matters

Earth rise over moonscape. The gravitational attraction between the two bodies causes a vertical displacement of the earth's oceans, which causes tidal movement.

Knowing the sizes and times of tides is every bit as important as getting an accurate weather forecast.

Tides are the alternating rise and fall of sea level with respect to land, as influenced by the gravitational attraction of the moon and sun. Tides generally move around the globe from east to west as the earth turns on its polar axis. Flood tides can be imagined as the crest of a swell circling the earth.

In all but the handful of coastal loca- tions where tide ranges are just about nil, tides can be the most important factor to consider when planning a seatrout trip. Understanding the timing and tide range can be the difference between returning to the ramp safely with your limit, and calling Sea Tow since you knocked off your lower unit.

Some 20 known factors influence tides, but the largest factor is moon phase. Other factors include coastline configuration, local water depth, seafloor topography, wind strength and direction, size and vol- ume of local rivers, and barometric pres- sure. Individually and cumulatively, these factors can alter the arrival times of tides, their range, and the interval between high and low water. Tides that occur around the new and full moon will be higher because the sun aligns with the moon to exert greater gravitational pull during those phases. The sun—solar bulges—is the second most important factor, and strong winds are often the most significant local factor. They can leave a flat that's rarely exposed high and dry at low tide.

Highs and Lows

Spotted seatrout occur prolifically in the inshore waters of both the Atlantic and Gulf coastal basins. An angler who trailers his boat from one basin to the other must deal with two fundamentally different tide systems, diurnal and semi-diurnal tides.

Diurnal tides bring one predictable tidal peak and one predictable tidal trough per day. Gulf Coast anglers see diurnal tides from the Florida Panhandle to the Mexico border. The fluctuations are rarely more than two feet, and generally only in areas with large, branching riverine watersheds. Their volumes of water contribute slightly to higher Gulf Coast diurnal tides. In the case of the Mississippi River, the massive volume of water actually offsets rising tides.

Fish don't often feed during slack tide, but you can catch trout on either the rising or the falling tide. Many Gulf anglers, especially along the central Gulf Coast, prefer the falling tide because the marsh grasses filter the

water and bait gets flushed from the marsh grasses. Flood tides are the best tides on many winter flats, because they allow mature trout to move up onto shallow, dark-bottom flats that have been soaking up the sun.

The U.S. Atlantic Coast has an orderly pattern of semi-diurnal tides, which bring two tide peaks and two tide troughs every day, one about every six hours. Often, the best fishing occurs at the start of the falling tide or beginning of the incoming tide. But

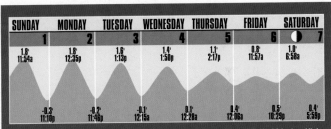

Above, Pensacola tide chart reflects the **diurnal** tides of the northern Gulf of Mexico. High and low tides occur once each day. The distance between the peak and valley shrinks as the days get farther away from a new or full moon. Below, Mayport tide chart reflects the southeastern Atlantic Ocean's **semi-diurnal** tides. Two high tides and two low tides occur every day. Their range is also determined by the moon phase.

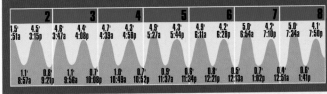

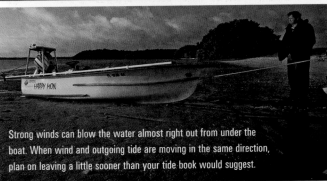

Strong winds can blow the water almost right out from under the boat. When wind and outgoing tide are moving in the same direction, plan on leaving a little sooner than your tide book would suggest.

along the Atlantic Coast and in some Texas areas, the bottom of an outgoing tide is often best because trout will concentrate in shallow depressions and dropoffs, versus being scattered across a deepening flat.

Prop scars on a shallow grassflat. By knowing what the tide is doing, boaters can avoid damaging fragile habitats. Pole or use a trolling motor if it gets too shallow to run.

You can set your watch by the tides. They occur about 50 minutes later each day. Be careful, as wind and other factors hasten or delay tides.

Some marsh areas, such as Lafitte, Louisiana, have very little tidal influence. Winds drive currents around fishy grass points.

basins. Here at the confluence of tidal rhythms, some days the southwest Florida Gulf Coast gets two high tides and some days just one. Some tides are a mixture of conflicting tides.

Some of the most famous seatrout fisheries in America are virtually uninfluenced by tides. Florida's Mosquito Lagoon, the Banana River and the upper Indian River Lagoon are three Atlantic Coast examples. A goodly percentage of Louisiana marshes don't fluctuate much due to tides, especially around Lafitte. In such places, water levels are largely determined by wind and local precipitation.

Generally, tide times change 50 minutes every day, corresponding to the moonrise 50 minutes later every day. A tide table or tide watch is handy, given the number of variables in tide prediction. SB

Some parts of the world experience "mixed" tides, and southwest Florida is a prime example. The Florida peninsula lies between the relatively shallow and small Gulf basin and the huge, deep Atlantic

Low Country tides can range more than 7 feet. Tides carry baitfish and shrimp through areas where trout wait to ambush their prey, but moving water isn't enough. Clarity and volume of water are important considerations. For example, a particular fishing spot can be highly productive on a day with a 5-foot, 5-inch high tide and a .5-foot low tide when the current is moving at 2 knots. That same spot is not productive at all on a day when the tide goes from 6-foot 6-inch high and 0.0 low and the current is 3 knots. There's just too much current on the day with the more extreme tide range. The strong current stirs up the marsh's muddy bottom and the silt particles move in suspension, clouding the water.

There are also times, during less extreme tides, when there is not enough current. If an average or weak tide flows in a southeast direction and the wind is blowing against that current the wind can have a stalling effect, which

know if it's clean enough to stop and fish. Dirty water clarity translates to poor visibility for the fish. If the tide is honking, and especially if the wind is stirring things up as well, seek out sand or shell bottom as far away from muddy areas

In dirty water, break out the metal. A weedless spoon trailing a scented soft-plastic curly tail will find fish.

as possible. Silt can carry for miles during strong tides and reduce water clarity even in adjacent sandy or shelly areas.

Carry detailed tide tables that give heights of each high and low tide and pay attention to weather and wind conditions before deciding

Tides range six feet or more in Low Country marshes. When the water's out, trout congregate in deep creek holes.

can turn fish off. It is fair to say that trout fishing is most productive in between moon phases that cause the the strongest tides and those which cause the weakest tides.

A good guide can look at the water and

where and how to target these fish. Realize that tidal aspects combined with other important variables are the fundamental factors in fishing conditions, and fishing success.

—Captain Peter Brown

Moon Phases

The sun's gravitational force on the earth is only 46 percent that of the moon. So, the moon is the single important factor for the creation of tides. But the sun is an important influence as is the centrifugal force created by the earth spinning on its axis. The moon pulls the water away while the earth's surface tugs back. The moon's gravitational pull is just slightly stronger so you get tides and not the canceling out of each other's gravitational strength.

Many experienced seatrout anglers avoid fishing during the full moon. The fish will often feed at night, and the huge high tides can spread them all over creation. New moons, on the other hand, bring brisk tidal fluctuations and dark nights. Often, fish feeding activity is predictably confined to the coincidence of moving water and optimal water temperatures.

Spring Tides

The gravitational forces of the moon and the sun both contribute to the tides. When the moon is full or new, the gravitational pull of the moon and sun are combined. At these times, the high tides are very high and the low tides are very low. This phenomenon is known as a spring high tide. They occur when the earth, the sun, and the moon are in a line.

SUN

Neap Tides

The sun and moon work at right angles during the moon's quarter phases, and almost cancel out each other's influence. But since the moon exerts more pull, you still get a smaller difference between high and low tides. These are known as neap tides. Neap tides are especially weak tides. They occur when the gravitational forces of the moon and the sun are perpendicular to one another (with respect to the earth). Neap tides occur during quarter moons.

Proxigean Spring Tide

The proxigean spring tide is a rare, unusually high tide that occurs when the moon's orbit approaches the earth (at its closest perigee, called the proxigee) and in the new moon phase (when the moon is between the sun and the earth). The proxigean spring tide occurs at most once every 1.5 years. SB

Fishing Neap Tides

Sun and moon at 90-degree angle to earth: Neap tides run slowly. Seek out submerged structure such as oyster mounds or dock pilings, and work methodically. Suspending plugs are great for "spot work."

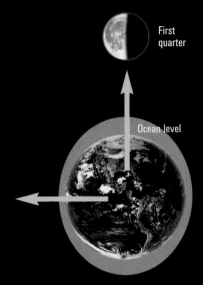

First quarter

Ocean level

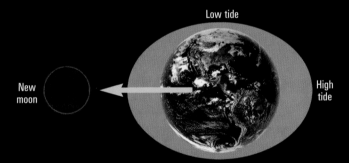

Low tide

New moon

High tide

Fishing Spring Tides

Sun and moon aligned with earth: Spring high tides can spread trout out all over creation. The bottom of the tide is a better bet. Work creek openings and the mouths of the guts that drain the flats with bait, flies or lures that match available forage.

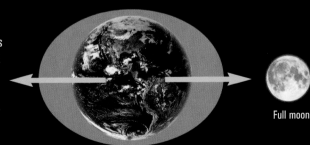

Full moon

CHAPTER 8

Structure

A number of different types of coastal ecosystems occur throughout the spotted seatrout's range. They include shallow, clear grassy lagoons and sounds such as Texas' Laguna Madre or North Carolina's Pamlico and Albemarle sounds. They include coastal estuarine delta systems such as where Florida's St. Lucie River and Indian River Lagoon converge, as well as massive muddy deltas such as the whole of Louisiana's "boot" that is sinking into the Gulf. They include complex spartina marsh systems, such as the Low Country marshes of Georgia and South Carolina. And they include open bay systems such as the Chesapeake. They even include structure well out on the continental shelf.

Spotted seatrout aren't too picky about habitat. You'll often find them where two types of habitat converge. Channel edges are a prime example. The channel itself offers a deepwater refuge when water temperatures rise too sharply or plummet. A shallow adjacent flat may offer ample ambush sites and an escape from larger predators such as porpoises.

Trout hang in diverse types of habitat. Seasons and water temperatures are major factors in habitat and depth preferences.

See DVD for more on fishing different types of structure.

Most places, you'll reel in
a little seagrass with your
fish. Above, pilings create
a crisscross of shadows
for trout to lurk in.

Soft Structure

Trout are primarily ambush feeders, not foragers. They cover themselves with seagrass. Your shadow will spook fish you never knew were there.

Emergent or submerged fish habitats don't necessarily contain hard structures. Superb camouflage allows seatrout to set up an ambush position or take refuge in soft mud near marsh grass, in seagrass, and around shoals and sandbars. Many fish, as well as reptiles and amphibians have light-reflecting cells containing pigments called "chromatophores," which are responsible for skin and eye color. When fish change hues or colors, the phenomenon is called physiological color change. Changes are triggered by hormones or neurotransmitters and may be initiated by changes in mood, temperature, stress, water color and surrounding habitats. Trout translocate pigment and reorient reflective plates within

chromatophores to instantly darken or lighten their spots to blend in.

Seagrass Meadows

Grassflats are the single most important type of vegetative habitat in most coastal

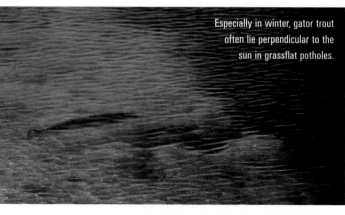

Especially in winter, gator trout often lie perpendicular to the sun in grassflat potholes.

estuaries. Because they bind sediments to the seafloor and filter out excessive nutrients, seagrasses are vital to water quality. They provide a complex cover for an incredibly diverse array of animals, from the lowly amphipod to the blue crab to the spotted seatrout. Almost every species we value as anglers spends some time in seagrass. Many cannot survive juvenile life stages without it, or find sufficient forage as adults. The entire foodweb is dependent on this type of soft, complex structure, down to the algae diatoms that are grazed from the blades by myriad crustaceans.

Thus, the vast majority of hours on the water seatrout fishing are spent over grassflats. Like most juvenile estuarine gamefish, and for that matter most reef fish, for the most part newly hatched spotted seatrout settle out in seagrasses or marsh grasses. But a key difference is that seatrout are closely associated with seagrass throughout their life histories. Their backs and sides are speckled by evolutionary design, to help trout to blend into these estuarine meadows.

It's as important to keep in mind how a trout feeds as it is to match the hatch. Unlike their close cousin the redfish, trout are more ambush feeders than forage feeders. Their bodies just aren't designed to roam. The shoulders and tail muscles aren't nearly as dense, and they lack the armor of hard scales that reds and other drums have. Instead, they lie low in potholes in seagrass beds and wait for meals to come to them. The prominent canine tooth or two teeth allows trout to latch onto prey and drag it back to the lair. If you have good light and a boat with platforms you can sight fish for individual trout. If the water is reasonably clear, target the potholes and their edges. Otherwise, work an area slowly and thoroughly with fan casts, and work all levels of the water column until you crack the code.

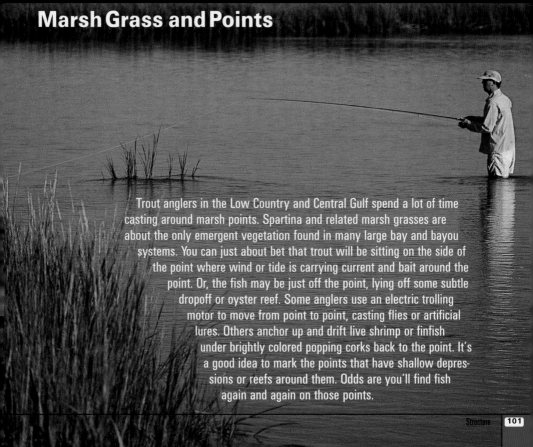

Marsh Grass and Points

Trout anglers in the Low Country and Central Gulf spend a lot of time casting around marsh points. Spartina and related marsh grasses are about the only emergent vegetation found in many large bay and bayou systems. You can just about bet that trout will be sitting on the side of the point where wind or tide is carrying current and bait around the point. Or, the fish may be just off the point, lying off some subtle dropoff or oyster reef. Some anglers use an electric trolling motor to move from point to point, casting flies or artificial lures. Others anchor up and drift live shrimp or finfish under brightly colored popping corks back to the point. It's a good idea to mark the points that have shallow depressions or reefs around them. Odds are you'll find fish again and again on those points.

Sandbars

Keep in mind that sediments settle out in different energy environments according to weight and shape. Many coastal areas have deposits of quartz sand, material that was eroded from mountain ranges by water. Rivers carry the material to the coast. Quartz sand is generally fairly dense and polished. Compared to silt, it takes powerful forces to move it. Therefore, you'll often find sandbars and shoals in high energy environments, such as the deltas that usually form inside inlets and passes, and on ebb shoals outside of them.

Sandbars block currents and give seatrout a place to lie in ambush without expending overmuch energy. They also can create a washtub effect that disorients baitfish and makes them easy targets.

It's not just a type of habitat that you look for, but a combination of favorable conditions. For example, because many sandbars lie just inside inlets and passes, and because incoming tides bring in fresh, cool water, these sand features can offer great summertime fishing.

Mud Flats

Some places, such as Louisiana estuaries, have little else to offer in the way of benthic structure than mud soft enough for a trout to wallow in. Oyster reefs offer cover and food. But usually, a trout will prefer to lie on the soft sediment surrounding the reef.

In summer, trout may avoid dark bottoms. But in winter, mud flats serve as the space heaters of the estuarine world. Dark bottoms absorb light and heat and then radiate the surrounding waters. Trout appreciate this warmth, and it jump starts the metabolism. Even old, fat, lazy trout develop an appetite as the tide pushes in over shallow mud. But just as importantly, the warmth invigorates forage such as shrimp and crabs that would otherwise lie dormant.

Gator trout are often caught on the edges where two kinds of habitat abut each other, such as a sandbar and a channel. Above, a wading angler enjoys the stealth advantage, as well as the ability to straddle such margins and work them methodically.

Trout are opportunists, and even in the dead of winter a fish may rise to a topwater plug. But when fishing the mud, especially in the winter, it's wise to use scented baits and work them slowly, so that they push up a little trail of mud. Small skimmer-style jigheads with scented soft plastics work extremely well. Soft-plastic shrimp fished under a popping cork will also ring the dinner bell.

Hard Structure

Oyster reefs, foreground, hold food and heat and offer cover. Mangroves, background, also attract forage, offer cover, and provide shade. Look for points where reefs and mangroves converge.

Trout aren't "reef fish" per se, but are attracted to structure both above and below the waterline, particularly where there's current.

Adult trout also orient toward hard structures such as oyster reefs, or to manmade structures such as docks, bridges, or gas and oil infrastructure. Trout are definitely a schooling fish, especially as juveniles and young adults. The larger fish are a little more independ-ent but you'll typically find them in loose congregations around structure, whether hard or soft. Often the best trout fishing will take place where natural and man-made structures converge. Some places hold trout only because of manmade structure, such as the oil rigs off of coastal Alabama.

Oyster Reefs

As living water filters and reef builders, oysters are the most important inverte-brate organism in most estuarine systems. A single Eastern oyster (*Crassostrea virginica*) can remove nutrients from the

water column at a rate of 60 gallons of water per day. Systems where these bivalves have been over-harvested and/or killed by freshwater discharges, such as Chesapeake Bay, frequently experience harmful algae blooms and anoxic "dead" zones.

Oysters build what are called "biogenic" shell. They put on armor by secreting complex proteins called conchiolin from the oyster's outer epithelium or "mantle." The proteins are a mortar that binds aragonite, a type of calcium carbonate that precipitates or "falls" through the water column, into a shell.

Scientist usually describe reef-building corals as "ramose" or branching. Habitats such as seagrasses and oyster reefs are described as "rugose," or wrinkled. Nature abhors a vacuum, and when oysters grow in a colony, myriad forms of life settle into the nooks and crannies between shells.

Oyster reefs provide the most complex structure of inshore habitats. Think of the surface area provided by all those shells heaped upon shells and the forage that lives there.

These organisms range from algae to micro-invertebrates to shrimp and crabs. Algae attract herbivorous mullet, which are a favorite meal for trout. The tiny crustaceans attract pinfish and other finfish such as blennies that trout also eat. And trout will of course snack on crabs, worms and shrimp.

Oyster reefs also trap warmth

reefs—reefs where the structure is created by the animals themselves. In this case, oyster spat usually settles on old shells which form a kind of platform for reef growth. If you fish around Florida's Amelia Island and step off the boat, your buddy will need a crane to lift you out of the mud. But if you look around, you see huge oyster mounds that must weigh many tons. Gradually, shells spread out and form a base wide enough to sit on top of the mud without sinking too far. Then the base grows upward and outward as the oysters succeed. An oyster succeeds by developing a shell of its own or by modifying a fossil

from the sun and radiate the surrounding water. For that reason, it's smart to target oyster reefs in winter, especially reefs surrounded by blankets of warm mud. Oyster reefs near docks, points and on the edges of channels are often most productive. The weedless wobbling spoon is the classic go-to lure, but soft-plastic jerkbaits rigged Tex-posed work well, as do topwater plugs. Be sure when casting to close the bail or stop the spool before the lure lands. Wind can make your line drift and tangle in the emergent oysters. Fraying and tangles are inevitable.

Boat Docks

Trout love boat docks, especially if there is another type or types of habitat close by, such as oysters or seagrass. In summer, they take to the shade provided by the docks. When feeding actively, they wait in ambush somewhere in a semicircle around

Not all docks are equal fish attractors. Docks that stand over debris from hurricanes and other storms offer a cozier environment. Natural structure, such as oyster reefs and seagrass, makes a dock even more alluring. A nearby creek may pour a buffet right through the pilings. And docks that extend out to the edge of a channel can be productive because of the proximity of shade, cover and a deepwater refuge.

Jetties

Texas jetties are world-famous for big trout, but they're not the only jetties that produce fish. During the fall mullet run, trout move out of the estuaries and into the passes and inlets along the Atlantic Coast. They're even caught outside along the beaches.

Work the open areas near boat docks as well as the structure and shade. Fat trout, above, often lurk nearby. Below, trout lurk around detached rocks and swirling water around jetties.

As one Texas veteran put it, successful jetty fishing involves "figuring the rocks out." Jetties should be explored slowly and probed until, like a blind man reading Braille, you know each pocket, nook and cranny. Look for rocks that stick out from the base of the jetties. Look for the rocks and deep holes that create eddies and swirling currents, or "inverted currents." You can bet that when the tide is moving, shrimp, croakers, mullet and piggy perch are going to hold in those eddies and deep holes. Trout and reds won't be far behind.

the end of the dock. They will move in and out on the tides, staying in comfortable temperature and depth ranges.

Soaking live baits and soft-plastic lures under popping corks works wonders around docks. Topwater plugs can draw fish out from under structure, but sidearm skip-casting soft-plastic baits with spinning tackle under the structure may be the deadliest form of dock fishing for trout. The lure smacks the water sideways and skips just like a shrimp or scared baitfish. This technique can be used under any sort of overhanging structure.

Favorite Texas baits include live shrimp or croakers on snapper rigs with 2 to 4 ounces of lead, depending on the current and the depth. Some jetties require getting down as much as 30 feet. Stronger currents are often better, but frequently the start of the tide triggers the bite. Also try vertical jigging over the deep holes along the jetties with a leadhead jig that's heavy enough to get down in the current and to the fish. SB

Mangroves: The Most Important Trees in Tropical Estuaries.

Most anglers associate mangroves more with redfish and snook than with trout. But although trout have more of an affinity for open water than those species, they often lurk near mangroves. Anglers most frequently catch trout near mangroves, on top of shallow shelves that run under the branches. The fish may be waiting in ambush or sunning themselves in the knowledge that the nearby branches will protect them from birds and larger predators.

The spotted seatrout's range is much broader than areas where mangroves occur. Typically, mangroves occur only in tropical and sub-tropical climes, along the southern half of both Florida coasts and along the coasts of southeast Texas. But as the planet warms, mangroves are clearly colonizing northward. They're now found in northeast Florida and even in Louisiana.

Three species of mangroves occur in Florida, the red mangrove (*Rhizophora mangle*), black mangroves (*Avicennia germinans*), and white mangrove (*Laguncularia racemosa*). Black and white mangroves are typically found higher on the shore face. Their primary ecosystem function is to secure sediments that would otherwise smother nearby grassbeds, and of course to give birds a perch. The red mangrove or "walking tree" is by far the most important for estuarine life.

Red mangroves grow along or in the water. These are easily identified by the snarl of reddish "prop" roots. Barnacles, algae, even oysters and clams cling to these roots, and an enormous variety of shrimp,

crabs and fish live in these root "condos." The roots also trap and recycle sediment and nutrients. Mangrove systems are of priceless importance to a wide variety of estuarine and marine life, including a variety of reef species, such as snappers and groupers. But seatrout utilization of mangrove cover is opportunistic, mostly related to foraging. When trout are near mangroves, work the points just as you would marshgrass points, either with bait under a bobber or methodically with artificials and flies. If they're laid up just outside the prop roots and overhanging branches, try to get the sun behind you and sight cast, or blind cast down the shoreline working your way in and out. SB

Skip casting under mangroves is effective for many species, including trout. Hook a big trout close to a mangrove and it may bolt for cover just like a snook.

CHAPTER 9

Artificial Lures

Spotted seatrout can be voracious, opportunistic predators or finicky sleuths. Topwater plugs go flying. Six-inch jerkbaits get swallowed whole. Popping corks sink like stones. But extreme heat or cold, or a surfeit of food, can make these fish the laziest critters in the shallows. The grassflat where you absolutely slayed them yesterday may seem as lifeless as a putting green the next.

When trout are biting, it's fun to catch them with different lures and flies. When they're not biting, the last lure you pull from the box may be the one you should have been fishing with since daylight. In the warmer months, it's a good idea to start with a topwater plug or popping bugs then go subsurface. Topwater plugs cast a long way, so they make good "search" lures. Spoons and swimming plugs are great for prospecting subsurface. Soft-plastic baits and suspending plugs, which are usually fished slowly, won't cover a lot of territory, but are deadly when fishing finite features such as dropoffs or oyster reefs. You should keep an assortment of each of these lure types in your box.

In many circumstances, proper lure selection will let you out-fish anglers using natural baits. A wide array of lures allows for matching the hatch, covering large areas, and making pinpoint, stealthy presentations.

See DVD for more on artificial lures.

Diving plugs seem to struggle downward and float slowly up like wounded baitfish. You can work them quickly, as a crankbait, or use a slow, tantalizing retrieve over likely spots such as grassflat potholes.

Fish-Fooling Devices

There's no doubt that at times and in certain scenarios live baits such as mullet or shrimp work best for seatrout, especially the big, smart sows. But bait isn't always available, and the reward in fooling a wild fish in its element with a skillfully presented artificial lure or fly is much greater. Plus, learning to fish with lures and flies allows you to constantly improve on your fishing skills.

Trout lures can be divided broadly into hard baits and soft baits. Hard baits include topwater and subsurface plugs and crankbaits, as well as spoons. Soft baits mostly encompass the plethora of soft-plastic shrimp imitators, jerkbaits and grubs on the market. But feather jigs also fall under this category. Flies fall in a category all their own.

Surface Plugs

Most avid seatrout anglers would rather catch trout on top than any other way. It's a visually exciting duel that requires snapshooter reflexes. Selection of type, size and color depends upon local conditions.

Tossing topwater walking plugs is a good way to focus on larger fish and cover lots of water. Generally, they work best in low-light conditions.

Cup-face plugs are called "poppers" or "chuggers." Like all topwater plugs, they're designed to act like a frantic wounded baitfish. Most lack the ability to move laterally, at least much, but some "hybrids" such as the MirrOlure Popa Dog "pop-and-walk." With pure chuggers, the retrieve is straight, and often very slow. The popping attracts the fish, but the strike usually comes while the lure lies motionless or bobbing slightly on the chop. Big fish often like a topwater fished very slowly, and that's why so many manufacturers continue to improve on classics such as the venerable Creek Chub Darter. Some examples include Storm Chug Bug, Rebel Chug-R and Pop-R, MirrOlure 44MR and the Trader Bay Trout Slayer.

Propbaits, plugs equipped with one or two metal propellers that turn on the surface like airplane props, also work well when you want to work the plug slowly but really want to make some noise. The classic is the Smithwick Devil's Horse. Others include the Heddon Torpedo and the MirrOlure 5M-28.

Far and away the most popular and arguable the most effective topwater

When walking the dog, experiment with different rates of retrieve and try an erratic retrieve if steady twitches won't draw strikes.

Walk-and-Pop

Walking the dog is accomplished with rhythmic twitches of the rodtip, alternating slack and tight line during the retrieve. There's nothing wrong with letting the plug sit for a moment between twitches. Below, chuggers make loud noises and throw water around. Longer pauses between chugs are usually important and can result in more hits.

In low light, try several color combinations before moving on. During such conditions, trout see the same spectrum of colors that you do.

plugs are stickbaits or "walking" plugs. Examples include the Rapala Skitterwalk, Heddon Zara Spook, MirrOlure Top Dog, She Dog and She Pup, Rebel Jumpin' Minnow and Lucky Craft Saltwater Sammy. The technique is called "walking the dog" because the lure resembles a hyper canine surging left and right while straining against its leash. Rhythmic twitches of the rodtip cause the lure to slash from side to side. When the bite is frenetic, you may want to walk the dog quickly and make the fish react for fear

of missing out on a meal. A slow, tantalizing retrieve may be the ticket when you aren't seeing much surface activity. Sometimes a big gator will lie under a motionless walking plug and wait to strike when the retrieve resumes.

Size and sound are important considerations when selecting a plug. First, keep in mind that big baits catch big fish, and that a schoolie trout can be so aggressive it will strike a plug that's bigger than its own body. But also consider the size of baitfish in the area, and try to match the hatch. Or, if the area is just thick with bait, throw something larger, something that differentiates itself from the individuals in the thick schools.

Sound is an important consideration, and you should pay attention to surface conditions and depth. Size of a plug is a major factor in determining splash and noise. In slick calm and/or super skinny conditions you may want to choose a very small topwater; in choppy conditions, a 10-inch walking plug with a couple of rowdy ball bearings inside the body may be the ticket. Several manufacturers put ball bearings in different numbers and sizes inside chuggers and walking plugs, which also add weight for casting distance. Prop baits are by definition loud, but since they spend a lot of time lying relatively motionless think of the propellers as fish calls. With chuggers, you can decide how loudly to fish a chugger by working the plug subtly or firmly.

An Eye for Color

Color selection is debated endlessly. Keep in mind that a trout's eyesight is extremely keen. A trout's eyes have a membrane called the *Tapetum lucidum* that serves to reflect light back to the retina, increasing the quantity of light caught by the retina. This membrane, which dogs and cats also have, vastly improves vision in low-light conditions. That's why your pet's eyes and the eyes of many fish glow in the dark. When the sun is high it may be uncomfortable for the fish to look up, and they can't see much more than a silhouette anyway. So, trout don't often feed aggressively on top in the middle of the day, and when they do the color of the topwater plug really shouldn't matter much.

As a general rule, use brightly colored plugs in low light or dirty water and black, silver or gold colors in clear water and high sun. But the exceptions are endless. Many baitfish change their hue in darker water, so a darker plug will more closely imitate a black mullet in a muddy tidal creek, for instance. SB

Surface Plugs

Topwater plugs include walking plugs, chuggers and prop baits. Select according to conditions. Generally, noisy plugs work better in chop.

Suspending twitch baits are for methodical work along grass edges, oyster reefs, dropoffs and other finite areas of cover.

Suspending Plugs and Crankbaits

(slow sinking)

Suspending plugs and suspending crankbaits have slightly negative buoyancy and are designed to sink slowly. Many of these plugs look like floater/diver slim minnows and have similar action. The term "crankbait" comes from the tight swimming action you get from a steady retrieve. Or, you can impart a darting twitch. Of course the lipped varieties will dive a little when retrieved so you can explore different levels of the water column. Suspending plugs are great to use around dropoffs and submerged structure such as oyster reefs. You can't cover much water with them, but they stay in the strike zone. Favorite suspending plugs and crankbaits include the MirrOdine, Yo-Zuri Crystal Minnow, a number of Rapala models, the Rat-L-Trap series, the Bagley crankbait series and the Sebile Stick Shad. Rapala also recently introduced the Sub Walk, a suspending plug that you work like a topwater stickbait, except underwater.

Sinking Plugs

Sometimes called "twitch baits," sinking plugs have negative buoyancy and better depth capacities. What they don't have are lips and much in the way of built-in swimming action. You impart a twitch or attractive dart, or simply troll the plug or swim it straight back to the boat. Popular models include the soft Corky series, the venerable MirrOlure 52M and the MirrOlure Catch 2000. Go to a sinking plug after the topwater bite winds down. Use these plugs along shorelines, or to cover open water.

Crankbaits can be fished at various paces, and with straight or twitchy retrieves. They excel along edges.

Crustacean hatches, baitfish runs and quick changes like barometric pressure or other weather conditions can trigger explosive feeding.

Diving Plugs

Floating diving plugs excel around oyster bars and pothole-pocked grassbeds. These slim, lipped, minnow-shaped lures look and behave amazingly like wounded slender baitfish. Models include the Rebel Minnow, MirrOlure L52MR, Cotton Cordell Red Fish, Bomber

One surefire way to nab a gator is to make the plug dive and resurface repeatedly over a sandy hole in a grassflat, or along an oyster bar as the tide carries it past.

The hookup ratio with diving plugs may be a little better on average than with walking plugs, but it is quite amazing how a trout can still

Diving plugs shine on pothole-studded grassflats. Make them wiggle down into those sandy holes.

Long 'A', and several incarnations of the venerable Rapala. Some diving plugs, such as the Rebel Jointed Minnow, are two-piece plugs that wiggle extra tantalizingly.

With a twitch, a floating diving plug wiggles down like a struggling fish, then floats back to the surface as having given up. The diving action often succeeds in tempting a recalcitrant trout out of its lair. Strikes frequently occur as the bait rises to the surface.

manage to avoid all those treble hooks. Some manufacturers have tried various hook styles to address the issue. For example, Rapala's diving plugs come with a VMC SureSet hook, which sports one larger hook on the trailing treble. The SureSet seems to work better; but no matter which diving plug you're throwing make sure not to wrench the plug away from a boiling fish. Reel down as you put firm but steady pressure sideways to the direction of the fish's head.

Give Props to the Blades

Like most inshore saltwater lures, spoon tactics were learned from largemouth bass fishing. The weedless Johnson Silver Minnow and similar single-hook spoons with weedguards may be responsible for more trout dinners than any other lure. They are timeless search lures, heavy baits that cast far but run shallow due to

their flat shape. You can fish them like a twitch bait or retrieve them straight, making them wobble over the tips of seagrass blades before dropping into potholes. Wobbling spoons also work well around oyster bars, and they skip easily and slip right under overhanging branches and docks. Adding a curly plastic tail enhances the lure's seductiveness.

Keep in mind that bright spoons can spook fish on bright days in clear water. If you want to fish a spoon in such conditions, try a black or red model. Popular wobbling spoons include the classic Johnson Silver Minnow, the Bagley Rattl'n Minnow spoon, Red Ripper and Capt. Mike's Weedless Willow.

Jigging spoons aren't commonly used for trout fishing, but lighter models work well in winter when the fish move into deep holes. Spinnerbaits have become the rage in redfishing, and trout will hit them. When fishing for an inshore slam, some anglers turn to the spinnerbait after they catch their trout because the lures are more likely to draw a strike from a redfish. SB

Jigheads

Jigheads come in various sizes, shapes and shank lengths. Heavier jigs obviously cast farther, but they don't land softly and are more inclined to bury in grass. Most jigs used for seatrout fishing in shallow water range from 1/8 to 3/8 ounce. When working deeper channels and holes, switch to a 1/2- to 3/4-ounce jighead.

The shape of the jighead has much to do with the lure's action. By using a flattened, skimmer-style jig, you can get away with a heavier jig in shallow water. The flat head causes the jig to settle down on top of the grass at a flat angle, where round or pointy headed jigs will plunge into the grass. Plus, the hook

Bucktails are classic. Skimmers excel in skinny water.

rides up on a skimmer jig, so it is not inclined to grab grass or shell. Other head shapes, such as the pompano, ball, bullethead and lima bean hop or dart through the water column. If you're fishing with a curly tail grub, you may want to choose a jighead that really plunges, so you can maximize the tail flutter.

Hair Dressing

Among "hair" jigs, the most common jig dressings include bucktail, saddle hackles and nylon. Often these jigs are spiffed up with shiny materials such as Mylar, Flashabou or Krystal Flash. Many anglers custom tie their own jigs. They can be sweetened with a bit of shrimp, or doused in one of the popular fish-attracting scents. White, yellow, brown and chartreuse are popular colors. Popular models include the Gulfstream series, Back Bone Skimmers and the Bagley bucktail series.

Most jigs find home in the corner of the jaw. For better penetration and easier releases pinch down the barb. Some advocate leaving the barb not quite flush with point.

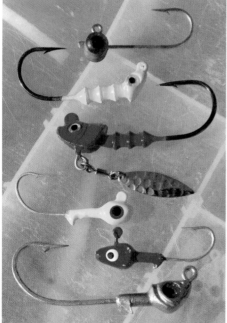

Measure the soft plastic against the hook before penetrating, and don't let the hook push out through the body short or it will sit in a long tear and could cause the tail to slip.

Good Scents

Pay a visit to the Berkley labs in Spirit Lake, Iowa and you'll meet a crew that serves as the wine tasters of the underwater world. Scientists test out new scents on these fish. Back to the chemistry set goes the scientist when a fish turns up its nose.

Don't be afraid to soak unscented soft plastics or hair jigs in the juice.

There are many scents on the market today that undergo rigorous lab and field testing. Increasingly, anglers are opting to sweeten lures with commercial scents instead of stopping by the bait store for shrimp. With most scents, you need to touch up your bait every 10 or 15 casts. The scent stays on longer if you leave hair jigs and unscented soft plastics in a Tupperware container to "marinate." Popular scent brands include Carolina Lunker Sauce; saltwater varieties include Crawfish, Menhaden Shad, Sardine, Shrimp and Crab. Berkley's Gulp! Alive comes in Squid, Shrimp, Crawfish, Mullet, Pogy, Peeler Crab and Bloody Sandworm. SB

Soft Baits

Bucktail and feather jigs deserve a place in every seatrout angler's tackle box. But despite their long history of success, innovations in soft plastics and similar baits have caused these classics to fall out of favor.

We've come a long way from the rubber worm and the pork belly. Today's soft-plastic and other soft lures such as Berkley Gulp! are products of serious research. They're designed for durability—to stay on a hook. And the scents are masterpieces of chemistry confirmed by laboratory and field experiments. They can be fished on a jighead, as jerkbait on a worm hook or even as a topwater.

Plastic Tails and Jerkbaits

Customizing options for soft-plastic baits are virtually unlimited. Plastic bodies can be placed on jigheads in lieu of hair. Choices include curly tails, shad tails and flap tails. The plastic bodies suited for jigheads are generally short, but some jighead manufacturers make long-shank jigheads for anglers who subscribe to the big bait, big fish theory. For example, the D.O.A. C.A.L. series offers long-shank jigheads that hold a 6-inch jerkbait without too much distance between tail and hook point.

Four- to 6-inch soft-plastic baits are often fished as weightless, weedless jerkbaits, or like Texas-rigged plastic worms, with or without a bullet weight. You can even use a syringe to blow air into the plastic body, so that it will float. Walking the dog with a soft-plastic bait is a deadly trout tactic, if only because trout bite them and don't let go. In some deepwater scenarios, a Carolina-rigged jerkbait can be deadly. The weight is pinned by two swivels a set distance up the line, which allows the jerkbait to float up tantalizingly from the bottom.

These days, most plastics are impregnated with fish parts or scented in other ways. Popular soft plastics or products made of other materials are made by D.O.A., Berkley, Pradco, Floriday's Fishing, Hogy, Hookup Lures, Bagley, Riptide, Old Bayside and Cotee.

The D.O.A. Chughead displaces water on the surface and below, and sinks level. Berkley Powerbaits and other soft plastics can be used on top or as jerkbaits.

Scented soft plastics can be rigged like natural baits and fished on the bottom or under a cork.

Lifelike Soft-Plastics

Fly tiers draw a distinction between impressionistic attracter patterns and imitative patterns. Because some inshore saltwater lures are much more imitative than others, this distinction is as useful when discussing fishing for the saltwater drum known as the spotted seatrout as it is when talking about a freshwater salmonid such as the cutthroat trout.

Down to the scent, some of the most imitative lures for shallow-water inshore fishing are made from soft plastic or materials of a similar texture. Designs mimic shrimp, crabs and a variety of baitfish. They

In the early 1990s, shrimp, crab and baitfish imitations appeared on shelves looking so real that anglers and trout fell hard for them.

can be rigged weightless and are excellent for sight casting in shallow, clear water. Or, you can fish them under a popping cork. Examples include: Sea Bay Shrimp and Crab; D.O.A. Shrimp, Crab, Baitbuster and TerrorEyz; Berkley Gulp!; Pradco Houdini Crab; Carolina Lures Sandflea; and Cotee.

Flies for Seatrout

Perceived difficulty prevents some people from learning to fly fish. Though fly fishing does require some practice, most experienced fly anglers are more than happy to share their experience. In truth, fly tackle is the most ver-

Fly fishing is challenging, but in the right hands, at least in shallow-water situations, the fly rod can be most effective.

satile of all inshore tackle. Fighting a fish on fly tackle is the most direct connection in fishing, and there's no better way outside of live bait to fool fussy fish.

Different lines—from floating to heavy-sinking—allow the fly angler to make lifelike

Bendback patterns, top, are great in the grass. The hook is protected by the wing. Below, the venerable Clouser Minnow is ever deadly.

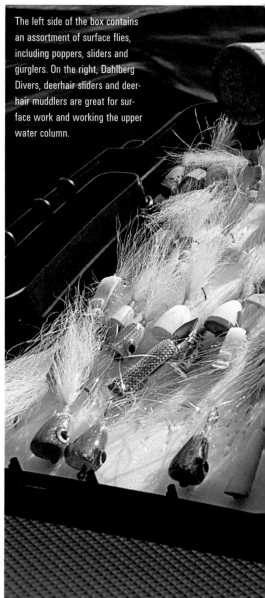

The left side of the box contains an assortment of surface flies, including poppers, sliders and gurglers. On the right, Dahlberg Divers, deerhair sliders and deer-hair muddlers are great for surface work and working the upper water column.

presentations to the fish throughout the water column. The flies themselves can be remarkably lifelike (imitative), or draw strikes just by being a general representation of a baitfish, or by splashing seductively on the surface.

Imitative patterns include crustacean patterns such as the S.L.S Shrimp or Merkin Crab, and baitfish patterns such as the classic Glass Minnow. These flies look so close to the real thing you could scare somebody by putting one of these patterns on your buddy's

shoulder when he isn't looking.

Attractor patterns include Lefty's Deceivers, Bendbacks, Norm's Crystal Schminnow, Glass Minnow and the Eat Me. Perhaps the quintessential attractor pattern is the Spoon Fly, which like its metal relative is weedless and shiny. Cork or foam popping bugs, deerhair bugs and sliders are the three primary topwater categories. Clever innovations of these basic patterns include the Crease Fly, Dahlberg Diver and the soft-foam Gartside Gurgler.

Perhaps the best all-around spotted seatrout fly is the venerable Clouser Minnow, which resembles any kind of baitfish or shrimp. It can be tied with weighted eyes so that it offers jig-like sinking characteristics. The classic SeaDucer, with palmered hackle body, is another time-honored trout pattern. Virtually any traditional streamer or bucktail pattern may be tied in appropriate sizes and color patterns to achieve results with spotted seatrout. **SB**

CHAPTER 10

Natural Baits

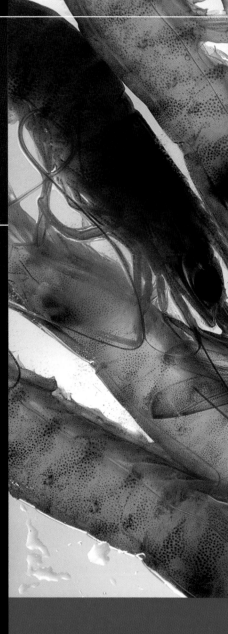

Y ou know an angler is serious about catching a mess of seatrout if an array of rods rigged with brightly colored popping corks is riding proudly along the center console. You can bet the livewell is full of bait. Fishing live or dead bait under a popping cork or "float" is deadly. The angler "pops" the cork to attract fish. The noise sounds like feeding activity which makes fish curious. In most situations, fishing bait under a cork is the most effective way to fish with natural baits, but certainly not the only method.

Some trout fishing involves chumming. A traditional chumbag can be used, or you can dice shrimp. But you may attract pesky opportunists such as catfish and pinfish. Live chumming with small whitebaits is a great way to conjure up a gator trout.

Freelining jumbo live shrimp, mullet, pinfish, croakers and pigfish is undeniably the most efficient way to catch a gator trout, especially if they're holding in a channel or around structure. But friskier baits, such as mullet, do a good job of covering a flat for you.

Some anglers feel naked leaving the dock without bait. Live or dead bait can save a tough day, and baitfishing tactics are a great way for the novice angler to start learning.

TROUT

See DVD for more on natural baits.

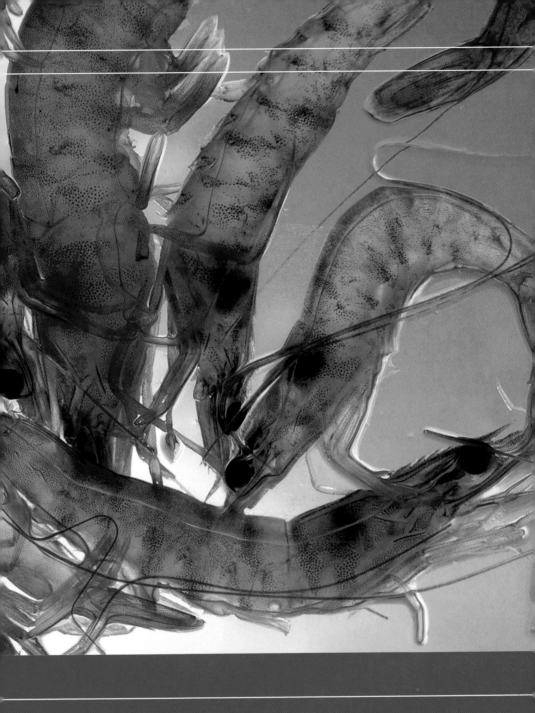

Live or fresh dead
shrimp are far and away
the most commonly
used bait for seatrout.

Trout Treats on the Menu

The big bait/big fish paradigm is especially real for trout. More gators are caught with live finfish than any other method.

As a general rule, juvenile and young adult spotted seatrout forage primarily on crustaceans, especially shrimp and crabs. Larger adults become more "piscivorous," which means they focus more on finfish in order to get more energy for the energy they expend feeding. But trout are rarely selective feeders, and there are huge regional variations to this generality. For example, trout of all sizes key on Low Country shrimp hatches. During one of those hatches you can float a finger mullet until dark and beyond and watch your buddy who is fishing with shrimp catch one trout after another.

Shrimp

The three species commonly caught and used for bait in both Atlantic and Gulf waters are brown shrimp (*Penaeus aztecus*), white shrimp (*Penaeus setiferus*) and pink shrimp (*Penaeus duorarum*). In many places their availability is seasonal, but shrimp are the year-round popular bait for spotted seatrout. During runs, anglers can catch all the shrimp they need with castnets and dip nets. Although seasonal availability of shrimp changes from region to region, generally live shrimp can be tough to find in the dead of summer and winter. Fortunately, over the last decade, researchers in Florida and Texas are discovering ways to raise bait shrimp that hopefully are free of diseases and thus safe to use in the wild for bait. These shrimp are just starting to become available in bait shops, and word is that they are larger, hardier and friskier than wild shrimp. The technology has the potential to create a regular supply of uber-shrimp and reduce pressure on wild stocks.

You can keep shrimp alive in a sophisticated livewell system, in a bucket with an aerator, or in a bait bucket. The problem with the bait bucket is that you have to leave it in the water to keep the shrimp alive, which makes long runs problematic.

When available, shell out the extra bucks for jumbo shrimp. They catch bigger fish and last longer where pinfish and puffers are a nuisance.

If you're fishing from a kayak or canoe and space is an issue, you can keep shrimp alive in a small cooler. A Styrofoam chest will do just fine. Fill the ice cooler half full of crushed ice. Wet about one section of newspaper with the saltwater from the live shrimp tank. Place the paper on top of the ice and make sure no ice is showing. Place the shrimp on the newspaper with no water. Replace the lid on the ice cooler and let the shrimp chill down. The shrimp go into some type of hibernation, but the second you return them to the water they come back to life. This method will last all day, even in hot weather, as long as the shrimp stay damp and chilled, and as long as they do not come in contact with the icy fresh water below them. Keep the lid on that ice chest and drain the water frequently as the ice melts. Separating live shrimp from the ice by storing them in a metal coffee can is another good technique. Again, no water.

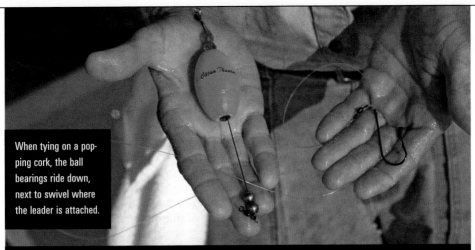

When tying on a popping cork, the ball bearings ride down, next to swivel where the leader is attached.

Fishing with Shrimp

Shrimp, live or dead, will catch trout. But live shrimp are certainly preferable. Shrimp are fragile. Avoid the major organs by hooking a shrimp through the horn or through the tail. Another option is up through the mouth and out the top of the head. Make sure you avoid the brain.

Live shrimp are usually fished under a popping cork on a light jighead or just a hook, but they can be freelined around docks and oyster bars, or fished with weights on the bottom in deep holes and channels. Dead shrimp can be used to tip jigs, or fished under corks and on the bottom with weights.

When sight casting to big gators on shallow grassflats, you should Texas-rig the shrimp to make sure it doesn't hang up in the grass. Bite off the tail flippers, run the hook down through the last section of the body and then bring the point back up into the body. SB

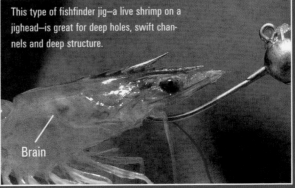

This type of fishfinder jig—a live shrimp on a jighead—is great for deep holes, swift channels and deep structure.

Brain

Finger mullet are frisky baits that cover water well. Make sure you keep the livewell lid closed or they'll jump out.

Mullet

Several types of mullet inhabit the nearshore waters where spotted seatrout occur. These include the striped or "black" mullet (*Mugil cephalus*), white mullet (*M. curema*), fantail mullet (*M. gyrans*), redeye mullet (*Mugil gaimardianus*) and Liza (*Mugil liza*). Some species interbreed and hybridize.

Adult mullet are herbivores and can be caught on hook and line only with small pieces of dough. Castnetting is the best way to fill a well. Some anglers prefer juvenile or "finger" mullet for baits, but even a small trout will attack a large striped or white mullet, especially if it is injured.

Mullet can be freelined or fished under a float. Hook a mullet through the lips or above the anal fin if you want the fish to stay on the surface. If you want to get the fish down, pin it through the lips with a jighead or fish it on the bottom with a knocker or Carolina rig.

Mullet strips, or pinfish strips for that matter, also make great trout bait. Simply fillet the fish so that the fillet tapers down. Remove bones but leave the skin on and hook the strip through the thicker, wider end. They are usually fished on a Carolina rig so that the flat strip can rise and undulate in the current. Beneath a popping cork is another good way.

Croakers emit a distress call that drives trout insane. They'll converge from all over the flat.

Croakers

Atlantic croaker (*Micropogonias undulatus*) and other small drums are prized by anglers seeking that trout of a lifetime. Like

Herrings and Menhaden

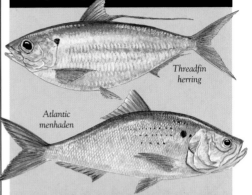

Threadfin herring

Atlantic menhaden

most drums, they have the ability to make noise underwater and their distress call attracts trout from far away, making them the go-to bait in dirty water. Croakers are hands-down the favorite and most controversial bait in Texas, but they're a pain to catch. Except when they school up on the beaches, you have to catch them one at a time with small hooks and bits of shrimp. If you wish to buy them, you have to get up pretty early in the morning to beat the crowds to limited supplies at Texas marinas. Some conservation-minded anglers worry that these baits are too effective, particularly on large, breeding sow trout.

Croakers aren't active baits, so they're usually fished beneath a cork and hooked through the back, on either side of the dorsal fin. In the surf, replace the cork with a small egg weight.

Pinfish and Grunts

Pinfish (*Lagodon rhomboides*), various perches such as the Chesapeake's white perch (*Morone Americanus*) and several

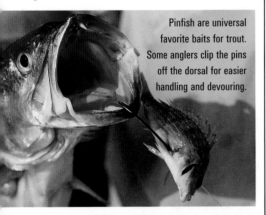

Pinfish are universal favorite baits for trout. Some anglers clip the pins off the dorsal for easier handling and devouring.

grunts (*Haemulidae spp.*) are prized trout baits in different regions. Pinfish are ubiquitous in trout territory, and are named as such because of the needle-sharp dorsal spines. The white perch is prized mostly in the Chesapeake region for trout fishing. Pigfish (*Orthopristis chrysoptera*), or piggy perch, are actually grunts. Pigfish are favorite baits in Texas, and they are certainly one of the most productive baits

The herring family is huge, but the most common herrings found in seatrout territory are the Atlantic threadfin herring (*Opisthonema oglinum*), the scaled sardine (*Harengula jaguana*) and the Spanish sardine (*Sardinella aurita*). Some anglers, especially along Florida's Gulf Coast, use a mix of oats, whetted wheat bread, fish oil, or canned jack mackerel for chum to attract a school, and then toss the castnet over it. The fish also strike gold-hook and Sabiki rigs. They aren't the world's hardiest baits, so try not to handle them more than necessary and store them in a well-oxygenated livewell system.

Although these baits can be fished under a cork, they are usually freelined, hooked through the nostrils, throat, or just ahead of the dorsal. As with mullet you can make the bait stay on the surface by hooking it just above the anal fin.

Atlantic menhaden (*Brevoortia tyrannus*) and Gulf menhaden (*Brevoortia patronus*) have quite a few nicknames, including bunker, shad and pogies. Juveniles are called "peanut bunker." They are incredible filter feeders and thus are vital to water quality. They are also loaded with fatty oils, which make them very desirable forage.

Menhaden are very fragile and difficult to keep alive. But trout love them, live or dead. Bunker also make excellent live or dead chum. Fish them the same way you would the herrings. SB

Frozen chum blocks or a home-made "potion" of fish oil, oats and ground fish attracts pinfish and herrings into castnet range.

for big trout in Florida's legendary Indian River Lagoon.

None of these fishes are strong baits so they should be hooked and handled carefully. The best place to hook these species is just in front of the dorsal.

Responsible Bait Fishing

The mortality ratio of trout is much higher when fishing with bait, period. There is so much concern over gut-hooking large female trout in Texas that the state has considered banning the use of croakers as live bait. There's a simple way to ensure that most of the fish you release will survive, and improve your landing percentage. Use circle hooks. These hooks almost always catch in the jaw. It's really rare to miss a fish with a circle hook and for the hook to find home anywhere else. SB

"Pancaking" a castnet is an art. Done correctly, throwing a net does not take tremendous strength, just good timing.

Obtaining Bait

Bait supplies can be seasonal, cut off by days of inclement weather or flat out exhausted by throngs weekend anglers. You may need to catch your own, and for most anglers that requires learning the art o castnetting.

Castnets range from 3 to 14 feet, measured by the radius of the circle of mesh or the length of the Braille lines. Mesh sizes depend on whether the mesh is a stre mesh or bar mesh. In general, they range from ³⁄₁₆-inch glass minnows and other very small bait to 1½-inch for large baits such as mullet and menhaden. Be mindful o state or local regulations which may limit net size or us on certain waters. Keep in mind that smaller mesh size mean that the net sinks more slowly, but the size of th lead weights in the s also determine sink r If you're netting fast baits such as finger r let, you need a net th sinks quickly. Bewar using a mesh size th is one size too large the baits. The net tu into a gillnet, and yo find yourself picking baits out of the net f hours.

Done correctly, ca ing all but the larges of nets does not tak enormous strength. There are a number ways to hold and throw a castnet, bu good form requires holding the net in a way that ensures its opening and allowin centrifugal force to "pancake" the net fo you. One of the easi and most effective ways is advocated the builder at Calusa Castnets (www.calusa.com). The company offers an instructional video, and their Web site has a concise, downloadable castnetting lesson. SB

Here's a Quick Look at a **Proven Technique**

1) Cinch the rope on your left hand if you are right handed, and vice versa if you're left handed. Place the net into your open palm and grip just below the horn.

5) You'll see two piles of lead, one high and one low. Grab the lead line where the high and low piles meet and place it in your teeth.

2) Pinch the net at hip level with your opposite hand and then grab it there again with the rope hand.

6) Drop the pile of net that is rolled over the thumb in your opposite hand and hold the net out at arms length.

3) Lift the net and split it in half.

4) With your opposite hand roll that half over the thumb of the hand holding the rope and net.

In the Calusa demonstration, the instructor compares the throwing motion to the motion a hammer thrower makes in a track and field event. You don't throw the net forward; rather you make a complete arc.

CHAPTER 11

Trout Tech

Fishing tactics for spotted seatrout are dictated by a combination of weather, water, financial means and to a lesser degree tradition. Genres include wading, drifting, poling, canoeing or kayaking, anchoring, and using an electric motor. Most genres have several styles. For example, to cover vast open flats, teams of Texas anglers practice in-line wading. Or, drift fishing can be modified or stopped with tools such as wind socks or spike anchors.

The most efficient tackle varies from tactic to tactic. By learning these genres of inshore fishing, you get to experiment with different rods, reels, lines, lures and baits. You open your knowledge base and improve your catch rate, maximizing the fun. The reward can be a lifetime of great fishing memories.

Trout tactics range from simple to sophisticated, relaxing to thrilling. You can just about customize your approach to fit the fishing preferences of captain and crew.

Unless he wants a Darwin Award, this angler might want to get out of the water. Top, trout often lie on shadow edges off shorelines.

Getting Wet, Wade Fishing

Simplicity, of course, is the greatest advantage in wading. In many places, you can catch a mess of trout or even a gator without a boat. You spend more time fishing and less time prepping, launching and cleaning up. But there are many tactical advantages as well. A stealthy wader can get much closer to a big wary fish than a boat-bound

gets about its near-death experience. For these reasons, experienced captains often use their boats as taxis and then have anglers get out and wade, even if it means slogging through water that's shoulder deep.

Wading automatically makes you vertically challenged, and working your bait from this disadvantage takes some practice. Twitching a plug or soft plastic now requires a vertical motion, which feels awkward at first. Plus, you just about have to set the hook with the rod behind your head, since it is already approaching the vertical position. Don't knock yourself over, or out.

When wading, never lift your feet entirely

Simplicity and solitude are pluses in wade fishing. Others include the ability to work an area thoroughly.

Wading angler plays a leaping trout. A small net is a good idea for landing fish out of the boat.

off the bottom, or a stingray may let you experience pain like none you've ever known. It's unlikely that a "stickfish" can get its barb into you if you nudge it with the toe of your bootie but the barb is almost guaranteed to find home if you step down on the ray. Kevlar "stickfish" boots, fishing's version of snake boots, virtually eliminate the threat, but they're not the most comfortable boots to wear.

If wading barefoot (not advised) or in lightweight wading

angler. A wading angler can fan cast 360 degrees and generally work an area more methodically with more line control. You don't have to worry about drift or the boat creeping up on your lure or bait. You can also stay with fish easier, while in a boat you may drift through the school and need to rely on a buoy or GPS system to find the fish again. You can change lures or flies without moving from the very spot where you think the fish are. And if you miss a fish, you can sit tight keeping an eye on the spot while the fish calms down and for-

booties, also make sure never to step back into your own "smoke." Your shuffling dislodges crustaceans, worms and baitfish from the mud or seagrass, and stingrays will follow you. Scientists call this phenomena, when one predator forages behind another predator's hunting efforts, "nuclear feeding." Anglers often call it, colloquially, "shadow feeding." Keep in mind that your trail may attract gamefish as well as stingrays, and the stingrays themselves attract flats foragers, such as spotted seatrout.

In winter, wading can be the most

Waders love suspending plugs, like the one that fooled this fat fish. They are designed to work slowly, high in the water column.

advantageous way to fish. Trout can get sluggish when the thermometer dips. An old adage about fishing soft-plastic baits for bass becomes especially true for trout. When you think you're fishing the (insert soft-plastic bait of preference) slowly enough, work it slower. It's difficult at best to crawl a soft-plastic bait through the grass slowly enough from a boat,

especially in a winter wind. Better to get out and wade, carefully. If you're wading in a new area, always test the bottom first to make sure it will hold your weight.

Careful winter wading begins before you even don your neoprene. Hypothermia can set on quickly in water less than 70 degrees, and even in water warmer than 70 degrees if the air

The Basics, Bells and Whistles for Wading

Some anglers insist on wading barefoot. But as our coastal waters become increasingly polluted and/or contaminated, the care-free wading we may have known as kids is being lost. A cut foot could mean a staph infection, or worse. So a good pair of wading shoes with hard rubber soles is important. Wading footwear ranges from Kevlar stickfish boots to soft-sided zip up booties to lace-up boots and flats sneakers.

Of course, the downside of wading is limited storage space. You can stick a handful of flies and lures in your hat and a spool of leader in your pocket. A better option is a combat wading belt that holds a watertight tackle box, leader spools, rod holder(s), lip gripper, landing net, stringer with float, water bottles and pliers. A bait bucket is essential if you're going that route.

Lightweight "flats" pants are a good idea when wading wet. They offer some protection from the sun, jellyfish and hydroids. SB

Obviously airboats aren't stealthy. This angler came prepared to wade, with a net, bait bucket, wading belt with extra rod holders and stringer. Below, good wading shoes, including "stickfish boots," are a wise investment. Bottom, wading belts with various capacities.

is cold. You should layer appropriately. Wear something that will insulate your core if you take on water. Be careful not to wear too much. You don't want to be too hot; sweating in your waders will lead to a cold ride home. And if the situation comes down to having to ditch your waders, you want to be wearing something you can swim in.

Waders aren't just for the cold season. Lightweight, breathable waders protect you from jellyfish, hydroids and the remote chance of catching one of the flesh-eating bacterias, through a scratch or open sore.

Capt. Bruce Shuler hoists his "personal best trout," a 32½-inch fish, with help from a gripping device.

Our place, Getaway Adventures Lodge, is on the Lower Laguna Madre, North America's only hypersaline lagoon. Except for a couple of manmade features such as spoil islands, channels and old gas pipes, the LLM is one huge shallow, grass-bottom expanse. From the poling platform, it all looks the same. But your feet will tell you different. Subtle contours—slight depth changes—are the natural structures that attract trout, and some of the biggest in the country at that.

When wading, let your feet be your depthfinder. Straddle the contour or edge along it, fan casting on either side. Concentrate most of your casts around the dropoff. Sometimes several contours run relatively parallel, but at different depths. That's where a team of anglers wading in a loose line formation can just about count on someone finding the fish.

—Capt. Bruce Shuler

Drift Fishing

Drifting is the most commonly used trout-fishing tactic. This style of fishing has had a tremendous influence on the evolution of inshore boats. When drifting, a wide, stable, shallow-draft boat is best. Contemporary bay boats, crossover skiffs and tunnel skiffs are designed as such. Flat-bottom boats work well for drift fishing. Kayaks are also well-suited for the tactic.

Drift fishing can be as relaxed, above, or as focused, right, as you like. It's a great way to cover wide swaths of water.

A boat with low gunnels, low console and flat bow profile will drift straight and slowly. The higher the gunnels, bow and console, the more the boat will "sail." But with the right tools and techniques, drift fishing for trout can be accomplished even in a 20-foot-plus, high-sided center console. You don't want to drift too fast to work baits and lures effectively, but fast enough to cover vast tracts of water until you find fish.

Besides boat length, freeboard and windage, your drift also depends on wind speed and direction and the tide, if any. The closer you are to a pass or inlet, the more tide will play into the drift.

Before setting up a drift, you need to do a little dead reckoning and anticipate where the forces will carry the boat and how quickly. Seamen identify wind direction from the direction the breeze blows. Current "flows to."

You may need to make minor adjustmen

With wind and tide opposing each other, you may not drift much at all. That's fine if you're working a favorite acre of a grassflat or piece of structure. You may even be better off anchoring and chumming, or using an electric motor to make headway.

Drifting is most challenging when wind and tide work together or against each other only at slight angles. Working a bait or lure properly is just about impossible if you're flying down a flat. You can slow your drift and set the angle

A drogue or "drift sock" deployed from amidships guarantees a sideways drift, allowing bow and stern anglers equal access to waters ahead.

o your drift.

of the boat as it drifts by lowering your outboard and turning it to one side or the other. But if it's really blowing, just lowering the outboard won't provide enough drag, and of course that's not an option in a canoe or kayak. Drogues, sometimes called "chutes" or most commonly "drift socks" can be deployed to slow any type of boat, and to keep it at angles that reduce hull slap and maximize casting area. Make sure you buy the right size to match the size of your boat. They range from 24 to 30 inches in diameter and cost from $35 to $200. The more expensive drift socks are adjustable.

You can deploy the socks in various ways, and get them to work in conjunction with the lowered outboard and a trolling motor. Deploy the anchor from the stern in a tail wind/current situation and you'll drift bow first. This angle is advantageous if you're working an

Making a controlled drift is imperative. A controlled drift allows you to work your baits, lures or flies naturally, through the most productive looking spots on a given piece of water. Drift socks facilitate control.

edge or shoreline or trailing a bait behind. When fishing an edge shoreline, you can optimize the bow angle for best casting angle by tying off on one side of the stern or the other. Just be careful if you're trailing a bait not to tangle with the drift sock or rope. By canting the outboard to one side or the other, you can turn the bow a little in either direction.

When fishing with bait under bobbers, drifting anglers have little choice but to fish in water they've drifted over. The sock slows the drift. Keep those baits back there, and have one angler pitch a lure updrift.

When you get in a school, hit "man overboard" on the GPS and go back to that spot.

The problem with the bow-first drift is noise. The sock will pull the stern down a bit and the bow may bounce, adding to any hull slap. Turning the boat sideways may (or may not, depending on the boat) be a little quieter and give more anglers a chance to work water in front and to the sides of the boat.

The great advantage in drift fishing is the ability to cover water, fast. But once you find fish you want to stay in them. Throwing a big anchor overboard more than likely will spook the fish. Various stick anchors such as a Power-Pole can stop you on the spot. But often it's best to drift through the fish, and then go back and reset the drift to move through them again. This approach gives the school time to settle down after a member or two departs mysteriously, thrashing spastically. A GPS unit is vital. Hit the "man overboard" button, and once you stop getting hits idle back updrift of the mark.

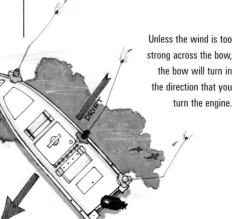

Unless the wind is too strong across the bow, the bow will turn in the direction that you turn the engine.

DRIFT

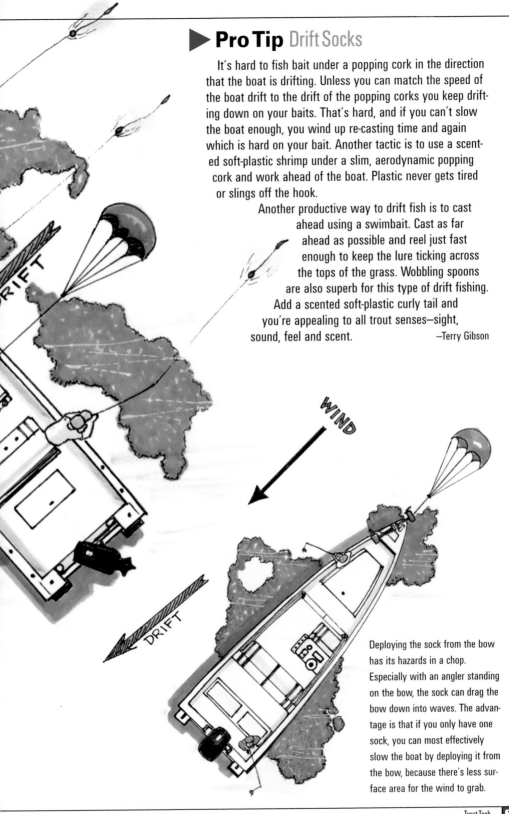

▶ **Pro Tip** Drift Socks

It's hard to fish bait under a popping cork in the direction that the boat is drifting. Unless you can match the speed of the boat drift to the drift of the popping corks you keep drifting down on your baits. That's hard, and if you can't slow the boat enough, you wind up re-casting time and again which is hard on your bait. Another tactic is to use a scented soft-plastic shrimp under a slim, aerodynamic popping cork and work ahead of the boat. Plastic never gets tired or slings off the hook.

Another productive way to drift fish is to cast ahead using a swimbait. Cast as far ahead as possible and reel just fast enough to keep the lure ticking across the tops of the grass. Wobbling spoons are also superb for this type of drift fishing. Add a scented soft-plastic curly tail and you're appealing to all trout senses—sight, sound, feel and scent.   —Terry Gibson

WIND

DRIFT

DRIFT

Deploying the sock from the bow has its hazards in a chop. Especially with an angler standing on the bow, the sock can drag the bow down into waves. The advantage is that if you only have one sock, you can most effectively slow the boat by deploying it from the bow, because there's less surface area for the wind to grab.

Electric Motors

Electric motors or "trolling" motors are getting quieter and more reliable every year. They are just about indispensable for most trout fishing that takes place in a boat, especially if you spend a lot of time drifting, or working creek holes and shorelines.

Most trolling motors used in salt water are bow mounted and controlled by tillers with handles that twist. Turn the handle clockwise and you go forward; counterclockwise is reverse. Speed is determined by how far you twist the handle. But the handle seems to attract fly line and tie granny knots in it. Plus, trout seem to have an annoying habit of biting when you take one hand off the rod to mess with the tiller. Manufacturers have solved those problems by developing electric motors controlled by remote electronics. A few anglers use stern-mounted, trim-tab mounted or lower-unit mounted electric motor systems. Obviously, these generate thrust from the stern. These systems are favored by diehard tarpon anglers and rarely used specifically to target trout. But of course they will work fine for that purpose.

Onboard charging systems allow you to keep your trolling motor batteries full simply by plugging in an extension cord.

Trout can be as spooky or spookier than bonefish, the difference being that a bonefish will shoot off a flat so fast it leaves a rooster-tail wake. If the electric motor makes a noise that a trout doesn't like, the fish will just slink off the flat without ever disclosing its presence. You may never know that you were looking for fish in the right place, just not quietly enough. By raising or lowering the trolling motor shaft, you can keep the prop blades just deep enough that they don't splash or cavitate on the surface and just shallow enough that they don't scrape grass or bottom. Also, when you change speeds, or switch into reverse, make the changes gently if possible. The spinning prop hits different pitches at different speeds. A constant or slowly rising or sinking pitch is less likely to bother a fish.

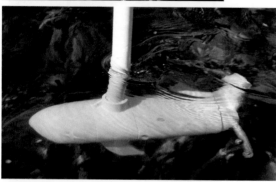

Keep the propeller unit just deep enough so that prop won't splash on the surface. Above, the captain operates the motor via remote control.

If you trust your partner, it's a good idea to fish tandem on the bow. This lets both anglers fish ahead of the boat while the trolling motor covers water.

FL 2576 M

Poling is an art, but not too difficult for the able-bodied to master. It is the quietest way, short of wading, to sneak up on big trout, and the best way to sight fish.

When poling over hard bottom, use the pointed end of the pole to push. It gets better purchase and makes less noise than the foot.

Poling

Poling is a tactic mostly associated with fishing for bonefish, tarpon, permit and redfish. But poling is a deadly tactic for trout, especially for sight fishing gator trout. Boat control, elevation and stealth are the primary advantages.

A clip atop or on the side of a poling platform gives the poling angler a convenient, quiet place to put down the pole and make a cast.

Most anglers who spend much time poling have their poling platform mounted over the outboard. The platform allows the poling angler to get above the glare by getting between the sun and the water. The angler on the platform will usually be the one to spot a big trout lying motionless in a pothole. A bow-mounted casting platform gives the angler holding the rod some elevation, too.

Poling angler works to keep the fish from getting behind the boat.

Learning to pole takes some practice, but it's not rocket science and you don't need to be built like a linebacker. Used properly, the pushpole only makes a gentle splash that's indistinguishable from a splashing baitfish. In hard bottom, use the sharp end of the pole. It is quieter. In soft bottom, you must use the foot. Assuming that there is no wind or current, a push on the starboard side will turn the bow to starboard and vice versa. Try to pole from one side only, because switching sides costs you momentum. Forward motion begins by placing the tip or foot just back as close to the boat on either side as possible, as long as the pole isn't so vertical that you can't get any leverage.

When poling use the clock system. The center of the bow is always 12 o'clock. Ninety degrees starboard is 3 o'clock and 90 degrees port is 9 o'clock. The outboard is 6 o'clock. When a fish is sighted, usually by the poling angler due to his/her elevation, angle and range are called until both anglers see the fish.

Especially when fly fishing, the poling angler must keep his wits about him. You must factor in wind direction, tide and whether the angler is right or left handed. Ideally you give your partner a downwind forehand shot so the backcast and delivery pass forward of the bow. You don't want the fly line coming into the boat or anywhere near the poling angler. Once it is spotted, neither the poling angler nor the angler in the bow should ever look away from the fish, even while the boat is being re-positioned. If the casting angler loses the fish, new coordinates must be relayed. Remember, no matter where the boat is positioned, the bow is always 12 o'clock.

Anchoring

There are a variety of scenarios that call for anchoring a boat to keep it in fishing position. When drift fishing, you may come across a school of fish and deploy a push-pole, Power-Pole or stick anchor to stay in the fish for the duration of the bite.

Other scenarios call for a real "hook." These include anchoring uptide of creek holes, marsh points, oyster reefs, bridges and other structure. As in drifting, you need to anticipate which direction the combo of wind and tide will cause the boat to drift as you let out scope. You don't want to sit over the hole or too close to the structure. Also, if facing into a sharp chop, make sure you let out enough rope so that the bow won't pearl. If the boat swings, deploy a second

Factor in the wind direction and the direction of the current before deploying the anchor or anchors above the area you want to fish.

Deeper basins such as this one surrounded by mud flats and mangroves are great places to anchor up and toss out baits.

anchor from the stern. Then set your baits out on the bottom or let your floats ride back to the edge of the structure or to the point.

Don't get too myopically focused on the water behind you. You may want one or more anglers to work ahead of the boat and along the sides, especially if there are holes ahead or dropoffs to the side. A jig with a plastic tail is good for this work.

Another trick, if you've got enough rope on-board, is to semi-continuously let out more scope so that you can keep fishing new water, once a spot seems played out.

Recovering the anchor can be difficult in strong current if it lodges in oysters or gets stuck under logs and debris. The best approach is to idle updrift of the anchor and try to slide it out from the direction it snagged. If it's really stuck, cleat off the line on the bow and drive around it 360 degrees. **SB**

Most but not all anchoring is done from the bow and fishing is done from the stern. Reverse should be used to keep the boat from drifting up on the anchor rope.

Time to anchor up. Catch a big fish like this and you may want to get out and wade the area.

CHAPTER 12

Gator Trout

Giant trout have a mystique that separates the big fish from the schoolies in ways that transcend sheer size. Many devotees are caught in a lifelong quest to improve on their personal best fish, or even a world record. It's a very cerebral quest, a lifetime of trial and error punctuated by success. The achievement is more than just a fish in hand; it signifies that you assessed the variables—wind, tide, atmospheric pressure, temperature—and put yourself in the right place at the right time with the right tackle. The quest of quests is to break Craig Carson's monumental achievement, the 17-pound, 7-ounce fish he caught May 11, 1995 on Florida's Indian River Lagoon, which stands as the all-tackle world record. The fish measured 39½ inches with an 18⅞ girth.

Carson and his dad were plugging a mangrove shoreline, and the fish hit the venerable red-and-white Zara Spook. It took 15 minutes to land, and six months for the International Game Fish Association to certify as a record, shattering an 18-year reign by a 16-pound fish taken by William Katko in Virginia.

Gator trout are one of the toughest of flats quarries. They are almost all long-lived females that have learned to identify the sound of hull slap, to study lures, and to slink off flats undetected.

Many experts use kayaks to target trophy trout, due to the stealth advantage.

Wading is the stealthiest and most methodical way to catch a fish of a lifetime. Capt. Ed Zyak with a 13-pound fish.

What's in A Name?

Gator trout are far more likely to inhale a topwater in low-light conditions, when they are sitting on top of the grass.

Large adult spotted seatrout are most often female fish. As usual, the female of the species is more deadly than the male, and in this case, bigger, too.

Big trout, those over 6 or 7 pounds are often called "gators." They are long and lean with wicked teeth and reptilian ferocity to match. They are also among the smartest, spookiest and most difficult fish to catch in shallow water, so bring your A game to this hunt. Some states, such a North Carolina and Virginia, award citations to anglers who catch a trout or other species of a certain size. Big trout can be studious of baits, both real and artificial. They have great eyesight. Excellent hearing and keen sensitivity to vibrations make them difficult to approach, much less fool. But when you fool one, the take can be spectacular.

Very few fish make more noise or throw more water than a big trout striking a topwater plug. Trout hit with a vengeance. A big trout flares its gills to suck prey back to its mouth in a powerful *whoosh*! Watching a gator suck in a streamer or jerkbait is one of the most exciting visual experiences in inshore fishing.

Location, Location, Location

The definition of a big seatrout varies from region to region, even sub-region to sub-region. But the record books show that you have a chance to catch a huge fish anywhere that the species occurs. That said, you'll have a much better chance in some waters than in others.

For example, a 6-pound fish would be a monster in Florida Bay or most places in Louisiana. But a few hundred miles away, in places such as Florida's Mosquito Lagoon or Louisiana's Lake Calcasieu where the environment is more conducive to breeding large trout, impressive fish start at about 8 pounds. There may be small genetic differences between the giant seatrout that live in some places versus the seatrout found elsewhere. Fish will typically be smaller in colder regions, where tough winters can limit food supplies and make the growing

Focus your casting on edges such as grass/sand margins and dropoffs. Big trout often lie on the shallow side of a slight depth change.

Top Gator Trout Destinations and Seasons

Texas: March/April on the Lower Laguna Madre.

Louisiana: February through April on Lake Calcasieu.

Mississippi: March through May, Horn Island.

Alabama: April and May, Little Lagoon.

Florida Gulf: April and May on Charlotte Harbor/Pine Island Sound.

Georgia: November on Wassau Sound.

South Carolina: November on Charleston Three-River Area.

North Carolina: November on Pamlico Sound.

Chesapeake Bay: September on Tangier Sound.

season shorter. Some estuaries, such as Florida's Indian River Lagoon and the Lower Laguna Madre in Texas, simply support more biomass. The food-rich, balmy environments with incredible habitats grow massive fish.

Just like where hunters try to encourage big bucks, management is key to growing big trout. Size regulations that limit the harvest of large spawning females help protect the fish with the best genes. But some states, most notably Georgia, where there is no upper end limit on trout, are possibly remiss on this management strategy. Anglers can encourage both larger trout populations and fish size by carefully releasing large trout. If you want to mount that trophy, take careful measurements and have an artificial mount made. These reproductions look better and last longer.

Tactics

Most big trout are caught at or near maximum casting range, especially when using artificials or flies. And long casts let you cover more water. When fishing with spinning or plug tackle, keep in mind the following casting considerations. Up to a point, longer rods—rods in the 7- to 8-foot range—cast farther than the 6-foot sticks designed for casting under overhanging vegetation and structure. The size and spacing of guides is another factor, but parabolic flex is the ultimate determining factor in casting distance. Most rods that cast a mile are fast-action rods, with maybe just the slightest wiggle in the tip.

Another factor is the line itself. Braided lines cast farthest—the lighter the braid the less the wind resistance. Trout are highly unlikely to break line, so gator hunters may scale down to 8- or 10-pound braid.

Elevation is always helpful when working a shoreline. You can peer down into potholes for outlines of fish, and gaze into the shadows.

When fly fishing, try to minimize the number and length of your false casts. False casts throw shadows across the water, and bad false casts smack the water at the start or end of the backcast. A fly line with an aggressive head helps load the rod and shoot.

Maximum casting distance becomes even more important when fishing from a boat. Noise carries much farther underwater and even the stealthiest vessels send out sound waves. Because of the elevation, you get a few more feet distance than a wading angler with similar casting abilities. You can also pick a spinning or conventional stick with a longer handle, since you don't have to worry about the rod butt splashing while fishing in a boat. Longer handles give more leverage.

Stealthy boat handling is imperative to get in range of gator trout. Next to wading or fishing from a canoe or kayak, the quietest approach is slowly poling a skiff downwind. This is the best way to sight fish, and the way that fly anglers catch their biggest trout. Drifting or using an electric trolling motor is effective if you cant the drifting boat to minimize hull slap, and operate the trolling motor on low speeds. If you spook one big fish, don't assume that you blew your shot at the only gator in town. Big trout are more solitary than younger fish, but they often lie 5 or 10 yards apart in small, loose groups on the flats. Stop, and let things quiet down for five minutes.

Bait Fishing Ethics and Tactics

In most situations fishing with live bait is a simple and effective way to catch a gator seatrout. Soaking shrimp, pinfish,

pigfish, croakers or mullet is a great way for a kid or a novice angler to tie into a trophy fish.

But fishing for large trout with live or dead bait is also controversial from a conservation standpoint. Many conservation-minded anglers contend that baiting makes it too easy for John Q. Public to

Trout eat shrimp throughout their lives. Buck up for the jumbos if you're fishing in gatorville.

catch and kill large breeders, the fish with the best genes. Gut- or tongue-hooking fish with bait is a frequent consequence that leads to increased mortality among fish that are released. These are serious concerns for both the size of the populations and the size of the fish. Big fish generate more eggs and contribute more significantly to the population structure. In some other fisheries, the most infamous example being North Atlantic codfish, long-term pressure on large fish derails natural selection to favor reproduction between smaller individuals. It's interesting to note that most of the state records for spotted seatrout have stood for a decade or more, despite many more skilled anglers on the water and tremendous advances in tackle, electronics, lures and boats.

No matter what type of bait you use, you should tie on a circle hook. In 99 percent of cases, the circle hook sticks in the corner of the mouth where it can be easily removed for a quick release. Second, fishermen have been using circle hooks for some 10,000 years, obviously for reasons not related to conservation. They are the most effective fish-catching style of hook. Unless you try to set the hook or use too small of a hook, a circle hook will almost invariably drive itself home and stay there. Just give the fish time to eat and then reel down until the rod bends.

Trout eat shrimp throughout their lives, but the big-fish, big-bait guideline is especially true for gator trout. If you're slinging a shrimp at 'em, make sure it's a jumbo shrimp. Good-size croakers, pinfish, pigfish and mullet are better baits for gators.

A common mistake when making the transition to fishing with circle hooks is to use a hook that's too small with too narrow a gap. A 2/0 or 3/0 J-hook would suffice for most finfish except for big mullet. Go up at least one number and probably two when tying

Gators on Fly and Light Tackle

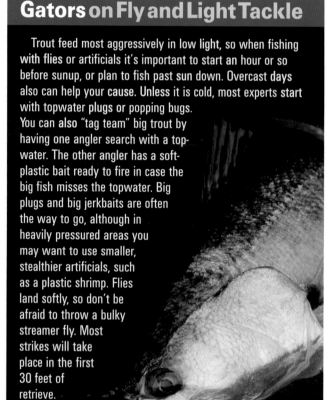

Trout feed most aggressively in low light, so when fishing with flies or artificials it's important to start an hour or so before sunup, or plan to fish past sun down. Overcast days also can help your cause. Unless it is cold, most experts start with topwater plugs or popping bugs. You can also "tag team" big trout by having one angler search with a topwater. The other angler has a soft-plastic bait ready to fire in case the big fish misses the topwater. Big plugs and big jerkbaits are often the way to go, although in heavily pressured areas you may want to use smaller, stealthier artificials, such as a plastic shrimp. Flies land softly, so don't be afraid to throw a bulky streamer fly. Most strikes will take place in the first 30 feet of retrieve.

Long, light fluorocarbon leaders are important when trout fishing in clear or even slightly stained water. Leader material that tests from 12 to 20 pounds is more than adequate. The fact that you get more strikes on lighter leaders creates a conundrum for anglers who fish where snook and other razor-gilled, rough-mouthed fishes occur. But if you're serious about catching a big trout, stick with the light leader. When it's cold, work plugs very slowly and let soft-plastic lures rest on the bottom for intervals between hops. SB

on a circle hook. A 4/0 or 5/0 hook is needed for 3- to 5-inch finfish. Use a 6/0 or even 7/0 circle hook when soaking big live mullet. Thin, light wire hooks are best because they allow the bait to swim relatively unencumbered, and they penetrate more easily.

Live baits can be freelined, tethered under an egg sinker with a knocker rig or Carolina Rig, fished under a popping cork or trolled. Dead baits, including shrimp fished dead on the bottom, strips of finfish and chunks of finfish can also be fished under corks, under weights or freelined in a chumslick. Live chumming is also effective. SB

For some reason spoil islands and spoil flats attract big fish. Work the potholes and the edges of the larger sandy patches.

Sight Fishing

Sight casting to big seatrout requires sunlight, so there's no reason to leave in starlight unless you want to do some blind casting first. Some of the best gator trout fishing in Texas and Florida occurs in the winter and early spring when the water is super clear and the fish creep up into the shallows to get warm. Odds are the best bite will take place midafternoon.

Sometimes you can catch a trout cruising along a shoreline, but usually they are laid up in potholes, sandy patches within grassflats. Cast at shapes that seem at all fish-shaped. Like reptiles, in chilly weather fish will usually orient their bodies to get maximum exposure to the sun. If there's a submerged log in a pothole turned broadside to the west on a winter afternoon it's probably not a log. Figure that the fish will face into the current. That's how you can deduce heads from tails.

When sight fishing for gator trout, use flies and lures that land gently. Fly anglers have an advantage in that they can throw larger offerings and still have it land softly. A favorite pattern is a white Woolly Bugger-type fly with monofilament eyes. Small jerkbaits and plastic shrimp rigged weedless are top conventional choices. SB

CHAPTER 13

Trout Down Deep

Spotted seatrout retreat to relatively deep water when the weather turns very cold or hot. They generally stack up in large schools around some type of structure. With the right presentations, you can catch a mess of them in one spot.

Deepwater trout fishing offers steady action and does not require tremendous angling skills. Fishing for trout schooled up over deep structure is a great way to introduce a kid or other new anglers to saltwater fishing. In fact, you can just about let the bait or lure do all the work.

Working the depths is an option just about everywhere seatrout occur, but deepwater fishing is practiced more in some places than others. Places where seatrout are considered both a "flats fish" and a "bottom fish" include Texas' Lower Laguna Madre, Alabama's Mobile Bay and the Chesapeake Bay. But folks in Florida and the Carolinas also resort to plumbing the depths when the weather demands it.

During extreme cold or heat spells, trout move into water as deep as 30 feet. A variety of tactics works for deepwater trout; most involve working baits and lures *slooooooowly*.

Even if the bay you're fishing doesn't get very deep, for summer fishing, scout out the deepest holes and grassflats for schoolie action.

Target Depths

Trout generally move into deeper water only during the summer or winter. They're trying to stay in a comfortable temperature range, and stay in oxygen-rich waters. In winter, winds and air temperature can cool the shallows and even down through middle levels of the water column, sending the fish below the thermocline. A properly tuned bottom machine can show temperature breaks by registering changes in water density.

"Plus, the oxygen gases off in the shallows so they must go deep to breathe." But trout and other species don't always have someplace to go to breathe. Dead zones, oxygen-poor areas caused by nutrient pollution, can trap fish between layers of anoxic water and cause fish kills. Dead zones are a huge problem for trout and other species in Chesapeake Bay.

Structure and Tactics

In deep water, seatrout act much more like reef fish than denizens of the shallows. On the flats, they can escape predators such as sharks and porpoises by hiding in the grass or swimming up shallower than the threat can go. In deeper water, trout are much more prone to predation. They usually, but not

At depths, trout become a much more structure-oriented species. A fishfinder becomes an even more invaluable tool in deep water.

Bridges and channels through pilings are favorite high-heat and extreme-cold trout hotspots.

In summer, trout also seek out deeper structure, in water that ranges from 10 to 50 feet.

"It gets hot up shallow," says Capt. Bobby Abruscato, an Alabama guide and *Shallow Water Angler* Central Gulf regional editor.

always, orient to structure when seeking more comfortable water temps and oxygen. There is also safety in numbers, and you will almost invariably find trout in schools when they're out deep. They may mix with weakfish, sand trout and silver trout. When looking for fish in the ICW or other deep channel, use your depthfinder to find structure on the bottom or ledges in the channel walls that afford some cover.

Deepwater trout aren't particular about the type of cover. In 2006, the *Shallow Water Angler TV* crew caught some chunky fish off an old Navy target sunk in 14 feet of water in Chesapeake Bay. Natural reefs, gas rigs, bridges, wrecks, ship channels and hurricane debris all attract fish.

"They still can't find over 200 houses destroyed by Hurricane Rita, but I found some of them in Mobile Bay," Capt. Bobby Abruscato says ruefully. "They're now summer and winter homes for speckled trout."

Anchoring just updrift of the structure is a traditional deepwater tactic, but you can also set up repeated drifts or use an electric trolling motor to keep in position. You may want to make a drift or two to make sure the fish are there before going to the trouble of deploying the anchor. If you have one, today's 4-stroke outboards are so quiet you may get away with using the outboard to stay in position.

Channel edges are great places to fish year-round. A chumbag, and a little live chumming will bring trout to you.

Sinking plugs such as this classic MirrOlure sinking twitchbait are great for working channel edges and other dropoffs.

Both artificial lures and live bait work well for trout suspended over deep structure. If you want to catch these fish on a fly, you'll have to resort to a heavy sinking line—400 grain or even heavier if the current is ripping. Mortar Clousers are the call.

With conventional tackle or spinning gear, heavy-head swimbaits shine in deepwater situations. Appropriate sizes range from ¼ ounce to 1 ounce, depending on the depth and the current. Swimbaits plummet to the bottom, but wiggle beautifully as they sink. You get more strikes when the lure is falling. Leadhead jigs rigged with scented soft plastics, or tipped with a bit of shrimp or cutbait also work well. And of course inexpensive "grub" tail jigs, or plain old bucktails, catch plenty. Just make sure to use a jighead with a hydrodynamic shape, or you'll have problems getting to the bottom. Leave those flat skimmer jigs in the box. Sinking plugs also do the trick. Lipped sinking plugs work best for trolling deep holes and channels.

A slip cork rig fooled this soon-to-be netted trout. Hooks won't catch in a rubber net and the rubber takes less protective slime off a fish. Below, a knocker rig works well for live or dead bait applications.

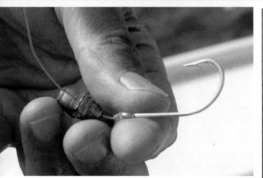

In winter, when you think you're working an artificial for trout slowly enough, slow down some more. Cold trout are lethargic.

A variety of live baits work around deep structure, and options vary from region to region. But don't count on being able to find live bait during the seasons when trout go deep. In many places, bait shops have trouble finding bait in the dead of winter or doldrums of summer.

Savannah, Georgia-based Capt. Scott Wagner says, "If you know what you're doing, you can catch more trout with soft plastics than you can with bait, but most Georgians only 'resort' to jigging in winter when nobody's selling shrimp or finfish."

Croakers are the favorite deepwater bait in Texas and along the Central Gulf Coast. Bobby Abruscato's favorite way to live bait for deep fish is to let the baitfish struggle under a slip cork. The bobber sits right on top of the sinker or swivel, but once the bait lands and begins to sink the line runs freely through the slip until a small bit of cloth or rubber stopper stops it. You set the cloth or rubber stopper at the depth you want the bait to drift.

A croaker is a bottom fish and will fight desperately to get to the bottom Once in the water, the croaker is strong enough to pull the line down through the slip cork, so you don't need much if any weight.

"That frantic croaker struggling to get to the bottom just over the reef really drives trout nuts," he says.

The slip rig is also popular in Northeast Florida and South Georgia, especially around bridges. In this region, anglers use shrimp for bait since the shrimp and trout drop down to 20 to 30 feet in the winter. You see boats running around ablaze with tall, thin red-and-white corks. Tall, thin corks don't put up as much water resistance as a fat round cork, which will drift too fast. The smaller, taller, thinner cork holds position better. Pre-made 18-inch leaders are sold in tackle stores, but really good slip corkers use at least 3 feet of light mono under a sinker. An ounce or so of weight is customary.

Other ways to liveline croakers and other finfish over structure include freelining or knocker rigs, and a Carolina rig with a minimal amount of weight if the current is strong. Live shrimp can also be freelined, fished under a small splitshot or fished on a jighead. Hook the shrimp through the horn. Mullet or pinfish strips work well under Carolina rigs. If you cut them thin enough, they flutter beautifully in the current. The downside of using dead bait is catching nuisance fish such as catfish, and dealing with pesky bait stealers such as pinfish, toadfish and blowfish. SB

Live finfish are better baits because bigger trout prefer fish over crustaceans, and because nuisance fish such as pinfish or catfish aren't likely to peck at them or eat them.

Hold a fish into the current before releasing it, so it can catch its breath.

Tricks for Locating and Catching Winter Trout

In winter, seatrout migrate into the creeks and rivers that feed coastal bayous and sounds of Central Gulf states, the Low Country, North Carolina marshes and creek systems of Northeast Florida and the Panhandle. In winter, trout also move into the canals dug for protective levees in Louisiana, and into residential canals along both of Florida's coasts.

"Around here, and this is true for most of the South Atlantic coast, the best wintertime trout fishing isn't found in the major rivers like the Savannah," explained Savannah, Georgia-based Capt. Scott Wagner. "The fish are in the rivers and creeks that flow into the major rivers."

In the winter, trout settle in dense schools in holes formed by the current flowing around oxbows. All kinds of debris litter the bottom of these holes, but they may lack any prominent structures. Big swirling eddies are a good sign. The swirling currents confuse bait and drive it downward.

"In the summer, when the fish move out into deeper water, they seem really keyed on a shrimp," says Wilmington-based Capt. Fisher Culbreth.

The same baiting tactics work in the deep holes and canals, especially a shrimp on a jighead. But artificial tactics are a little different for wintertime fish.

"When you think you're working that jig, plug or swimbait slow enough, work it slower," says Wagner about sluggish winter fish.

In Alabama and Mississippi, anglers simply let a soft-plastic jig drag along the bottom as the boat drifts through the holes.

"Old-timers call it 'do-nothing fishing,'" explains Mobile-based Capt. Bobby Abruscato. "They go out in their wooden skiffs and just stick the rod in the rod holder and wait for it to bend. I couldn't believe it would work, but I went along one day and those guys just made a fool out of me. They were catching 10 fish to my one." SB

CHAPTER 14

Surf Fishing

In the summer or early fall, spotted seatrout move out into the surf or "littoral" zones. Surf fishing is a dance with the waves, the rips, even the advance and retreat of the beaches themselves. In some places, Texas especially, the arrival of trout along beaches prompts the deployment of divisions of surf buggies down to the beach. Along the placid beaches of the Central Gulf, trout chase croakers and other bait in the suds between the beach and first sandbar. Anglers fishing bait—"croaker soakers"—as well as pluggers, catch 'em up.

Baitfish runs also draw trout out through inlets and passes. The most spectacular is the fall mullet run along the Atlantic Coast. Millions of mullet file out of the rivers and sounds and move south along the beaches, drawing every imaginable predator into the littoral zone, from estuarine fish such as seatrout to pelagic species includ-ing sailfish. Trout lie under the schools of mullet and pick off scraps of baitfish wounded by bluefish, Spanish mackerel, jacks, sharks.... Most of these fish are big, big enough not to be mistaken for bait.

Surf fishing is much more than a day at the beach. It's liberating. Brilliant sunrises, wave dancing and frenetic action occur where land, sea and sky meet.

Some places anglers can drive right down to the beach of choice. Make sure you lower the air pressure in your tires and avoid sharp turns, or you may get stuck.

The Littoral Zone

Most beaches in trout country from southernmost Texas to New York are "depositional" beaches, fed by rivers. They may differ in amount of wave energy, as well as their makeup, or sediments. These factors can have important consequences for trout fishermen.

Most Atlantic beaches are comprised of quartz sand eroded from the Appalachian Mountains and polished shell fossils. Along

east central and southeast Florida beaches, reefs are often adjacent. The snow-white beaches of Florida's west central, Big Bend and Panhandle beaches are almost pure quartz. Same for eastern Alabama. Close to the Mississippi Delta's influence, the beaches contain more clay and other organic material, hence the dark color and frequently roiled water despite little wave energy. Texas beaches benefit from rivers and from the slow erosion of dunes.

Central Gulf Coast beaches are usually calm with shallow grassbeds and oyster

Early morning is usually when you find trout in the first gut. Structures, such as shipwrecks, background, may also attract fish.

reefs. The Georgia Coast faces southeast—away from most Atlantic wave energy— and is protected by a broad segment of the continental shelf. The famous Georgia barrier islands have little inlets that the locals call "sloughs," and these complex systems of sand banks hold plenty of trout. Surf fishing along these beaches doesn't feel much different than wading a giant bay.

Most Atlantic beaches are much more exposed. It can get pretty rough for relatively long durations in places along Florida's Gulf Coast, Alabama's Dauphin Island and the Texas Coast.

Surf fishing success begins with the ability to read water well. Waves, wind, rips and backwash give the impression of chaos, when in reality the elements create structure and conditions favorable for seatrout feeding. A particular beach may or may not be produc-

Currents swirl around sand-spits, confusing bait and offering lazy trout lying in eddies an easy meal.

The surf zone is arguably the most fascinating and definitely the most dynamic of habitats where you can catch trout.

tive depending on water clarity and whether the sand teems with life.

The lower beachface is home for tiny invertebrates, about the size of a pinhead, which are the primary forage for juvenile surf fishes, such as spot, croaker and mojarra. Larger "infauna" include mole crabs, a.k.a sandfleas (*Emerita spp.*), bivalves such as surf or "coquina" clams (*Donax spp.*) and a variety of worms. Sandfleas become readily visible in the surf zone when they "pop" up out of the sand to filter algae from the water as it recedes from the beach. A beach with popping fleas and brightly colored clams is likely to support strong populations of croakers and other surf fishes that trout eat. Trout may snack on a sandflea from time to time, too.

Receding waves can carve little depressions out of the beachface, and rivulets form that sometimes drag beach-dwelling organisms off the lower beachface. Bigger fish stack up around these "rips," plumes of turbid water running more or less perpendicular to the beach.

Rips are generally stronger when they roll off steeper beaches. The undertow may be just strong enough to carry food into the trough immediately adjacent to the beach. Especially on the latter part of the incoming tide or the start of the fall, the first trough is likely to hold seatrout. They may hold right along the dropoff, waiting for croakers and such that have ridden waves onto the beachface to fall

Top Surf Spots for Trout

Alabama: Orange Beach
Season: summer

Florida: Talbot Islands
Season: summer/fall

Georgia: Ossabaw Island
Season: summer

Louisiana: Grand Isle
Season: summer

Mississippi: Chandeleur Islands
Season: summer

Texas: South Padre Island National Seashore
Season: summer

Spits often form around inlets and passes. Trout often follow baitfish migrations out along the beaches. Focus on dropoffs and shoals. Below, sand spikes are a must for a family outing.

Surf fishing for trout can get down right athletic. It can involve hikes, dead sprints to busting fish and challenging swims from bar to bar.

back off with the undertow. Trout may also use the beach to corral migrating baitfish such as mullet.

Really strong rips may dig a trench through the bar or bars. Trout often stack up where the rip carries food across the bar or in the trench between bars.

Tactics

Most anglers who target trout in the surf leave the beach with wet, sandy feet. There are two kinds of surf anglers, the passive and the active types. The passive type probably has a cart and is content to lob out baits to different ranges and have a seat. Then there is the peripatetic beach walker/surf wader. If you are one of the latter, avoid plowing into the surf so that you don't spook any schools of fish close to the beach. Sometimes, you can catch fish from the dry sand; do even better by stay-

ing high on the beachface to avoid casting a shadow. Some surf fishing requires total immersion. Texas anglers think nothing of swimming from bar to bar to get flies and lures in the zone. Florida anglers targeting trout during the mullet run wouldn't put a big toe in the water because of the large sharks chasing mullet up onto the dry beach.

Just about everywhere trout occur, rising water temps in the beginning of summer draw baitfish such as croakers, glass minnows and sardines out of the sounds and onto the beach. Sometimes trout give away their location by attacking these baitfish on the surface. This activity usually attracts squadrons of birds such as gulls from far away. If you see diving birds, fish under them. If there are no obvious signs of feeding, look for baitfish and stick with the schools. On those glassy summer mornings, look for the "sizzle" nervous baitfish leave on the surface, and sniff the wind for fish oil.

Sometimes the signs just aren't there. You have to work the surf zone methodically. Whether using bait, lures or flies, it's usually best to start by covering the trough, concentrating on the little rips and runouts, then work the bars.

Live baits, such as shrimp and finfish, are also an option when you're wade-fishing. The major problem with live bait is transporting it. If it's calm enough, you might try a floating bait bucket, but that can be cumbersome. Or you can use a floating bait net, consisting of nylon mesh suspended by a foam ring.

One of the most successful ways to find trout is to put out a live bait in the trough, under a cork if it's calm or under a knocker or Carolina rig if it's choppy. Croakers excel in this zone; their distress calls attract fish from long distances. Live mullet, pinfish, sand perch, mojarra and pigfish also work well in the suds. If all you have is dead bait, a big, stinking piece of cut mullet, menhaden or ladyfish—popular surf-fishing baits in the Carolinas—will do the trick, although you're likely to hook a shark or a ray. Various adaptations of the venerable fishfinder rig work best for dead bait. Let the bait sit while you set out another bait on the first and second bar. **SB**

Surf Tackle

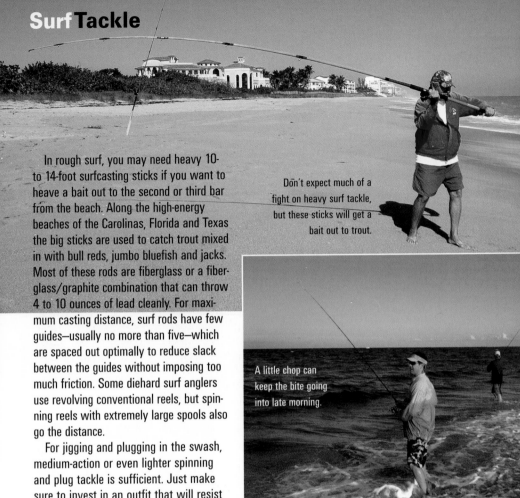

Don't expect much of a fight on heavy surf tackle, but these sticks will get a bait out to trout.

A little chop can keep the bite going into late morning.

In rough surf, you may need heavy 10- to 14-foot surfcasting sticks if you want to heave a bait out to the second or third bar from the beach. Along the high-energy beaches of the Carolinas, Florida and Texas the big sticks are used to catch trout mixed in with bull reds, jumbo bluefish and jacks. Most of these rods are fiberglass or a fiberglass/graphite combination that can throw 4 to 10 ounces of lead cleanly. For maximum casting distance, surf rods have few guides—usually no more than five—which are spaced out optimally to reduce slack between the guides without imposing too much friction. Some diehard surf anglers use revolving conventional reels, but spinning reels with extremely large spools also go the distance.

For jigging and plugging in the swash, medium-action or even lighter spinning and plug tackle is sufficient. Just make sure to invest in an outfit that will resist the cruel inflictions of sand and salt. Keep it lubed and wash it down.

Fly rodders can get away with an 7 or 8 weight in calm conditions. In strong wind, or when throwing a big popper, step up to a 9 or 10 weight. If there's a chop, switch to an intermediate sinking line or even a sinking line if it's really rough. Some devoted surf casters use double-handed fly rods descended from the Scottish Spey rod tradition. You cast these 11- to 14-foot rods overhand, and with foreshortened shooting heads a practiced hand can manage 130-foot casts. With such a long rod, the tip extends over the shorepound so the waves can't drag the line as easily.

Leader length and strength depends on water clarity and whether toothy critters such as mackerel and bluefish are present. Unless fishing with a popping bug, use fluorocarbon. Fifteen-or 20-pound-test is ample for trout. If you're heaving lots of lead with surf sticks, you need a 50-pound shock leader as long as your rod plus a few wraps around the spool. It acts like a rubber band when all that torque is applied.

For the mobile angler, terminal tackle includes an assortment of jigs, soft-plastic tails, topwater plugs, suspending plugs and crankbaits. If you're casting into wind, heavier, more streamlined lures such as swimbaits work well. For the surf caster, terminal tackle may include pyramid sinkers, spider sinkers if it's rough, barrel swivels and Kahle or circle hooks.

A wade-fishing belt allows you to carry the most essential items, such as long-nose pliers. SB

CHAPTER 15

Charts and Electronic Navigation

A paper chart gives you a mental picture of the area you intend to scout for seatrout. Take special note of the chart's legend, which matches symbols to structure and bottom types, including shell, grass, oysters, shoals and other trout-holding features. These days, you can also get an electronic, even 3-D picture of the area you're exploring, thanks to satellite-based global positioning systems (GPS) and chartplotting systems.

GPS relies on a system of satellites orbiting around earth that transmit microwave signals that enable a receiver to determine its longitude, latitude and heading. The best of these machines offer color screens and fish-finding sonar functions.

The Coast Guard requires guides to get an Operator of Uninspected Passenger Vessel, or "6-Pack," license. The test requires you to learn dead reckoning and chartplotting.

Running in the dark without an electronic chartplotter requires familiarity with area hazards. Take it easy, and make sure your navigation lights work.

The Technology

The greatest technology in the world is your brain. Knowing how to use a chart and a compass to find your way home will prove the most valuable skills you've ever learned on that day when the machines fail. Always carry a compass and a waterproof chart.

Charts are more than navigation tools. Some explicitly point out trout hotspots. They also note fishy features.

There are several good books on the subject of navigation and most boating safety courses teach the basics. To get your captain's license, you must demonstrate an ability to plot courses and navigate via compass and chart.

Charts

Charts are useful for navigation and for fishing. Good charts depict channels and topographical features such as grassflats, oyster bars and mangrove/marsh habitats. Don't overlook the little channels leading through flats or up to them. These may be favorite places for trout to hide during the heat of the day or in the winter. Look also for indications of broken marsh, small islands, oyster bars, sandbars and sloughs.

The more you fish an area, the better you learn where to fish given the various combinations of winds, water temperatures and tides. Having a float plan, and sticking to it, will help you catch more trout. That said, never leave fish to find fish.

Start by breaking out the chart and the tide tables. If you have high water early and the weather is warm, plan on working the skinny, skinny flats, submerged marsh points, or the backs of large bays. Falling tide spots include deeper grassflats and the sloughs that connect or divide them. Also search out points with good tidal flow running around them. Keep in mind that complimentary winds can hasten a falling tide and make it fall much farther than predicted.

Florida Sportsman Communications Network offers waterproof backwater charts with popular trout waters marked "TR." Hotspots for other species are identified as well. Locations are matched with colored dots that indicate which seasons offer the best action in that particular area. A star indicates that fishing is good year-round.

Florida Sportsman fishing charts identify popular trout fishing areas. Above, binoculars and a radio are fish-finding devices.

This angler's fish-call hat may be lucky, but careful research and practice put him on this gator.

Good charts also mark boat ramps, marinas and fuel stations for boats on the water. Some even list services offered by the marinas, and give telephone numbers so you can call ahead to find out when they're open, if they have fuel, or if they have a certified scale in case you land a potential record. In this age of extensive cell phone coverage, the number is also handy in case you break down and need a tow.

Keep your chart handy, both on and off the water. Most fishermen are happy to share valuable fishing information. You may run into a helpful brother or sister of the angle while filling up or running inside for ice. Make sure to preserve your charts by storing them in a dry compartment. For more information on Florida Sportsman Fishing Charts, visit www.floridasportsman.com. For information on aerial photograph fishing charts, call Standard Mapping Services, (888) 286-0920.

Live Satellite Photos

It's pretty hard to get lost with gargantuan reference points such as Tampa Bay's Skyway Bridge. But satellite imagery can help you find fishing spots near urban landmarks.

www.googleearth.com, www.terraserver.com, and other satellite map/imagery Web sites. Actually, with a home computer, you can study new water in great detail, down to individual features such as oyster reefs. With the click of the mouse, a map of the U.S. appears. Just

You can now see something of an area you've never even fished, thanks to web-based satellite imagery programs such as move the cursor to the location you want to explore and keep zooming in by clicking the mouse until the habitats you want to see are

FLORIDA

GULF OF MEXICO

TAMPA

Zoom in on Your Favorite Spots

Google Earth and similar technologies are easy to use. Start by clicking on the region.

TAMPA

TAMPA BAY

Click on the water body.

Chartplotters

Chartplotters are no replacement for a chart and a pencil, but these machines offer an electronic chart display that show your position and can be used to create waypoints. When fishing a new area or area that you are still learning, a chartplotter is just about indispensable. When you buy a chartplotting GPS unit, you can also buy GPS mapping software for a given region. The charts are uploaded from a data card or "chart chip." A tracking function shows exactly where the boat has been, making it simple to retrace your propwash, even in the dark. The chart should depict manatee signs and channel markers that may be hard to see at night or in driving rain.

Even when fishing water that you know like your palm, a chartplotter helps you stay in fish. Some tell the exact tide stage throughout the day. Some have temperature gauges that measure the temperature of the surface water. If you tune the depth and gain (sensitivity) prop-

clear. You can print out these images and lay them over a paper chart. Or there's an even more high-tech way to take advantage of this technology. Fugawi offers a Google Earth plug-in for Marine ENC version 4.6. Doubtless more companies will offer similar products and the technology will become more and more refined. Connect to the Internet, select waters and the software will pull up and save the corresponding Google images. You can run the images parallel to the chart. The program works on PCs and PDAs with a GPS connection. SB

Today's chartplotter/depth sounder systems allow you to run both functions side by side.

erly, GPS units with sonar capacity will read temperature breaks, too. And when drift fishing, you can hit the "man overboard" button when you start getting hits. After you drift through the school, just return to that mark. (Sure beats tossing out an anchor or a buoy.)

Don't be afraid of technology or costs. Running these units isn't rocket science, and units appropriate for backcountry fishing run from $400 to $1,100. Just make sure the unit is "sunlight visible." Color screens are also much easier to read. Think about visibility when you mount the unit. Install it where you can read it standing or sitting, but so that it doesn't impede your line of sight. SB

SKYWAY BRIDGE

TAMPA BAY

Click and click again until you see the area of detail down to the flats and other fishy features.

CHAPTER 16

Destination
Trout

From Maryland to Texas, spotted seatrout are a leading cause of excitement and enthusiasm among recreational anglers. Understanding the seasonal migrations, peak fishing months and habitat preferences throughout the year will help vacation planning and focusing your search. Except at the northern end of their range, there's never a bad time or place to catch trout.

License requirements vary from state to state, as do creel and size limits. If boating, be sure that your vessel and safety equipment are up to Coast Guard specs. Also make sure you're read up on current fisheries and boating regulations. Ignorance of the law is no excuse in court.

The following chapter suggests some favorite destinations, but is not meant to be exclusive. Thanks to trout, we have so much water to explore.

The better you plan and prepare, the more likely you are to come back to the ramp safely, under your own power, with a few fish to show for it. That said, many gators are caught on spur-of-the-moment roadside wading expeditions.

Fishing itself is an exercise of freedom. Finally getting on a plane is a moment of elation.

Surf fishing for trout in Texas should be on every angler's "bucket list." Working a topwater through the swash, you'd swear that trout hit harder than bluefish.

Trout on the Map

The Central Gulf and Low Country marshes are better known for massive populations; Florida and Texas are better known for trophy trout.

Virginia

North Carolina

South Carolina

Georgia

Mississippi

Alabama

Louisiana

Texas

Florida

ATLANTIC OCEAN

GULF OF MEXICO

Spotted seatrout live in almost every kind of inshore habitat and some off-shore locations from northern Mexico to New Jersey. (Weakfish, a close cousin, become more common on the Atlantic seaboard from Georgia to Rhode Island.) Seatrout spend most of their lives very close to where they first settled as tiny juveniles. In the northern extent of their range only are seasonal migrations apparent, such as the movement of Chesapeake Bay trout to North Carolina sounds in late autumn. Seatrout are loyal to specific spawning aggregation sites, so good trout fishing water, if cared for, remains good trout fishing water.

Seatrout behavior differs slightly from region to region, as do the size ranges of subpopulations. Suitable angling tactics also vary significantly. In much of the species range, drifting 3- to 4-foot-deep

Marshy creeks become trout holes in winter.

flats is a common approach spring, summer and fall. Waders catch their share of fish, where the bottom is hard enough for it. And surf casters score in many places during the summer months. A few anglers use bonefish/permit tactics and pole after big trout hunkered down in potholes. It's sight fishing at its toughest, due to the trout's wariness in shallow water.

No matter where you fish for trout, a live bait under a popping cork is dead-ly, as can be a plastic shrimp or jig dan-gling under a cork. Spoons are universal prospectors. Topwater plugs draw exciting strikes. Flies fool big fish laid up shallow. There's no shortage of places to catch trout, or fun ways to catch them. Here are some state-by-state best bets.

TEXAS

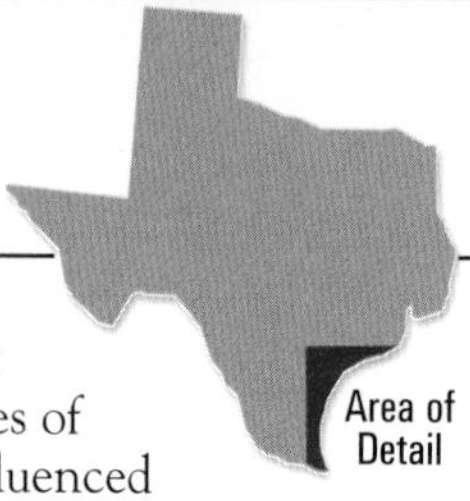

With almost 3,400 miles of tidally influenced coastline, Texas offers a lengthy and diverse fishery. To the south, the Gulf of Mexico and lagoons lap against desert. North and eastward, the setting consists of marshes and bayous. The central coast also offers vast bays that teem with seagrasses and oyster reefs. A few coastal rivers and canals also contribute to the seatrout fishery. Top spots include Baffin Bay, Galveston Bay, East and West Matagorda bays, Copano and St. Charles Bay, Sabine Lake and the Upper and Lower Laguna Madre.

Southernmost Texas is subtropical. Caribbean blue water laps at the beaches of massive barrier islands and South Padre Island National Seashore, which may offer the best surf fishing for trout in the country.

Area of Detail

It doesn't sit well with Texans that the current world record belongs to Florida. If and when a Texas angler breaks that record, that angler may be nominated for President of the Republic of Texas.

San Antonio Bay

Texas

Port Aransas

Corpus Christi

Gulf of Mexico

Baffin Bay

Padre Island

Laguna Madre

Lower Laguna Madre

Brownsville

Thanks to sound management, trout fishing is a Texas tradition that will live to thrill the next generation of anglers.

Matagorda Bay

Trout ought to be the state of Texas' mascot.

Best Bet

Most Texas coastal water bodies offer great trout fishing, and some of the biggest gators ever caught came out of the Lone Star State. But the Lower Laguna Madre gets our nod as the best Texas trout fishing destination because it boasts the most records and the best management. In 2007, local anglers successfully fought for a regional limit of 5 fish and a length measurement slot that protects large breeding females. As North America's only hypersaline lagoon, the LLM is also an ecological wonder worth visiting for the scenery and wildlife.

LOUISIANA

Area of Detail

Many Louisiana anglers consider the spotted seatrout a superior fish to redfish, especially for eating. According to Sea Grant researchers, spotted seatrout or "specks" are targeted by more recreational fishermen in Louisiana than any other salt-

water fish. According to Marine Recreational Fisheries Statistics Survey data, recreational fishermen have harvested an average of 13.6 million speckled trout from Louisiana waters annually, between 1999 and 2001.

Louisiana marshes still produce more trout than any Gulf or Atlantic estuarine system.

Louisiana trout vary greatly in size average from region to region. In the Houma/Golden Meadows area, or up around Lafitte, you're almost guaranteed to catch a mess of small, tasty trout. But catching a gator is pretty rare in those areas. Lake Calcasieu and Lake Charles are better known for big fish, and this is attributed to genetics, deepwater refugia where they can escape winter's cold, and larger, more abundant forage.

Vermilion Bay

Atchafalaya Bay

Lakes Calcasieu and Pontchartrain are famous for gator trout on par with this one.

Best Bet

Lake Pontchartrain gets the nod because it is an excellent fishery in its own right and because of its great comeback story and its proximity to New Orleans. Oyster/clam dredging ended several years ago. Once filter feeders were left to do their jobs, the muddy and polluted lake rebounded, and seagrass sprouted again. Many of the big trout are caught in deep water, including the two deep passes that connect Lake Pontchartrain with Lake Borgne.

MISSISSIPPI

Hurricanes Katrina and Rita, in the same year, razed coastal Mississippi, but the fishing quickly rebounded. Much of the year, the coastal marshes of Biloxi Bay, Back Bay of Biloxi, and the marshes along the east bank of the Mississippi Delta offer the best trout fishing. Pascagoula marshes also teem with trout, as do the Cumbust Bayou marshes. Bang's Lake and the Bay of St. Louis are open water venues.

Other top spots include the oyster reefs in the Mississippi Sound, around Pass Marianne Light south of Pass Christian;

Area of Detail

Back Bay of Biloxi

Bilox

Gulfport

Mississippi's barrier islands may be sinking, but the fishing sure isn't. A trip out to these islands is a journey well worth making.

Some of Mississippi's best trout are found in the delta marshes.

oyster reefs off Long Beach; off the Pass Christian Small Craft Harbor; the big stretch of oyster reefs behind the small islands on the north side of Deer Island across from the Isle of Capri Casino in Biloxi; and near the entrance of the Back Bay of Biloxi at the mouth of Fort Bayou.

Mississippi

**Biloxi
Bay**

**Deer
Island**

Pascagoula

Gulf of Mexico

During the winter, you may want to hunt ducks in the morning until the marsh ponds warm up enough to get trout feeding. These anglers know to take advantage of afternoon sun.

Best Bet

Razed by hurricanes, starved of sediment by human alterations to the Mississippi River and beset by rising sea level, Mississippi's barrier islands are disappearing. But they are fishing as well as anyone can remember. Petit Bois, Horn, Cat, Ship and the Chandelier islands offer superb surf and flats fishing for big trout, mostly in spring, summer and fall months. Winds and seas make it tough to get out there during winter, but mothership operations overcome that obstacle. They may operate less frequently or not at all during winter. Check with local operators. These remote places offer a great shot at trophy trout.

ALABAMA

Area of Detail

Trout are caught throughout Alabama bays. Fishing effort focuses on piers, inshore artificial reefs, oyster reefs and coastal rivermouths and the petroleum and gas drilling rigs in Mobile Bay. Surf fishing off Gulf beaches is productive in warmer months. Marshy or grassy areas, oyster reefs, inshore artificial reefs, rock jetties and shoal areas all hold trout. In the late fall and winter, trout either move into deep water in Mobile Bay or up rivers and into deep holes, dropoffs, or channels. On the western shore, the Dog and Fowl rivers are

Wade fishing around Alabama's oyster reefs is usually productive, especially with suspending plugs.

famous for winter trout runs. The Mobile-Tensaw river delta is also a classic cool-weather fishery.

All sorts of methods are used for trout in Alabama. Livebait fishing with shrimp and croakers is most popular. But jigs, spoons and plugs all have their place in this fishery. Best months are late March through April as the fish feed voraciously prior to spawning.

Mobile Bay offers diverse trout habitats, from man-made deepwater structure to oyster reefs and "duck ponds."

Alabama

Bayou La Batre

Mississippi Sound

Dauphin Island

Trout appreciate that Mobile Bay managers return oyster shells to the water for restoration's sake.

Grand
Bay

Mobile

Mobile
Bay

Best Bet

The oyster reefs of Mobile Bay near Dauphin Island hold large numbers of trout throughout the year. But they get red-hot April through August as the fish gang up to feed before the spawn during the summer months. The bite peaks in late spring, and the biggest fish are caught then as well. Spoons, plugs, jigs, suspending lures, and live baits fished under corks all get the bite.

Fort
Morgan

Dixey
Bar

Gulf of Mexico

FLORIDA

Area of Detail

Florida's Gulf Coast is known for huge numbers of trout, and plenty of nice fish. Florida's East Central coast is "gator alley."

Florida

Almost every inch of Florida coastline supports a healthy seatrout population. Only the Intracoastal Waterway in Broward and Palm Beach counties is no longer conducive to abundant trout populations.

From coastal salt marshes of the Big Bend and Panhandle, to the big bays of West Central Florida to the southern Everglades, to the nearly landlocked lagoons of Florida's Central Atlantic coast. Subpopulations of trout in Florida are managed differently from region to region. Seasonal closures are in place,

and the limits are higher in some regions than others. Check local regulations before you fish.

Ten-pounders are rare along Florida's Gulf Coast, but the lion's share of big fish are caught in the Indian River Lagoon, Banana River Lagoon and Mosquito Lagoon. Like the Florida strain of black bass, for various genetic and foodweb reasons these fish get huge.

Trout are always on hand to get Florida anglers excited. Schoolie action on both coasts is usually red-hot.

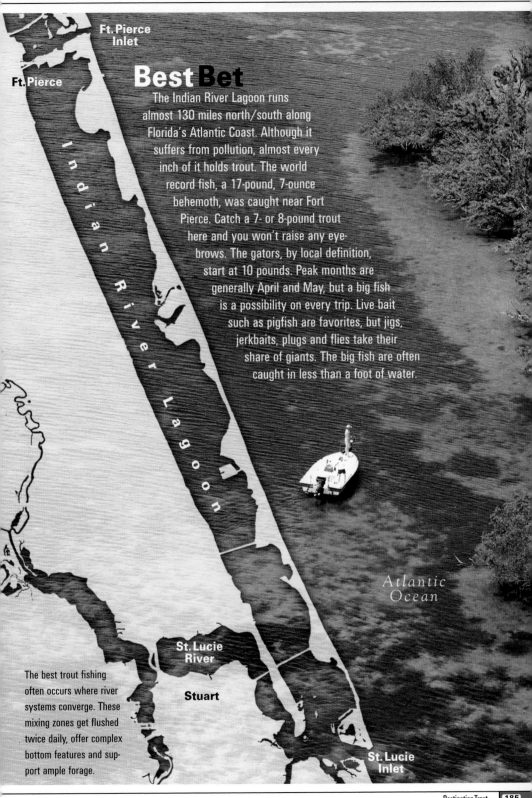

Ft. Pierce Inlet

Ft. Pierce

Indian River Lagoon

Best Bet

The Indian River Lagoon runs almost 130 miles north/south along Florida's Atlantic Coast. Although it suffers from pollution, almost every inch of it holds trout. The world record fish, a 17-pound, 7-ounce behemoth, was caught near Fort Pierce. Catch a 7- or 8-pound trout here and you won't raise any eyebrows. The gators, by local definition, start at 10 pounds. Peak months are generally April and May, but a big fish is a possibility on every trip. Live bait such as pigfish are favorites, but jigs, jerkbaits, plugs and flies take their share of giants. The big fish are often caught in less than a foot of water.

Atlantic Ocean

St. Lucie River

Stuart

St. Lucie Inlet

The best trout fishing often occurs where river systems converge. These mixing zones get flushed twice daily, offer complex bottom features and support ample forage.

GEORGIA

Area of Detail

Most of Georgia's coast is protected from development. Teeming marshes produce possibly the largest population of seatrout along the Atlantic Coast.

Georgia

Much of Georgia's coastline is undeveloped and protected from development. It's so wild it's easy to get lost, whether you want to or not. Almost every inch of it is productive trout water at some time or another. In the spring and summer, the fish stay out near the sound entrances, either in the sounds or in the sloughs along the beaches. Inside, almost any marsh point or grass

Georgia is known for big numbers of trout as well as the state's vast, beautiful marshes.

island with good current running along it will hold fish. Live shrimp is a favorite bait, but jigs and soft plastics let you cover more territory.

In winter, trout move back into creeks that feed the main rivers such as the Ogeechee and Altamaha. In fact, the best fishing of the year usually takes place in November when the fish begin migrating from the sounds into the backcountry. There they seek out deep holes where the creeks turn, or lie on the bottom of 300-year-old agricultural ditches that nature has reclaimed. Most fish are caught on soft-plastic bodies stuck on jigheads. In winter, bounce soft plastics along the bottom as slowly as possible.

Altamaha Sound

St. Simon Island

Jekyll Island

Savannah

Best Bet

If you're after a trophy, there are better places to go. If you want to catch a pile of trout, put Georgia on your mind. The Peach State's estuaries produce incredible numbers of trout. As a destination, Savannah just can't be beat. The area offers excellent fishing close to one of America's most beautiful and fascinating cities. No one area is that much better than another. Pick a sound, such as Altamaha, Sapelo or St. Catharine's Sound. Action peaks in late October through November.

Atlantic Ocean

The Georgia coast exudes a fascinating, inviting strangeness, where unique natural and cultural resources blend in an exotic mash.

SOUTH CAROLINA

Area of Detail

Throughout the Low Country, the best trout fishing takes place during the cooler months of fall and winter, as trout migrate back up coastal rivers.

South Carolina's trout fishery is similar to Georgia's fisheries—lots of small fish and lots of gorgeous salt marsh and oak hammocks. Here, too, the fish concentrate in the lower reaches of the rivers, in the sounds and on the beaches during summer. Marsh points and submerged and emergent oyster reefs all hold fish.

In fall, trout migrate back into rivers and take up residence in the deep holes. Top spots include the Three Rivers area, where the Ashley, Cooper and Wando Rivers meet near Charleston. The marshes near Hilton Head and the Broad River marsh systems also hold millions of trout.

Popular tactics for trout fishing in South Carolina are region-wide favorites.

South Carolina

Good-size "roe trout" are caught along the beachfronts in last spring.

Beaufort

Hilton Hea Island

You find plenty of popping corks, and in winter slip corks fly brightly on rods standing upright in vertical rod holders. But jigs, jig-and-cork combos, even top-water plugs and spoons are commonly used for South Carolina seatrout.

Best Bet

It isn't done as much as in the old days, but in late spring South Carolina's beachfronts hold some really big trout, at least by Low Country standards. Anglers search for sloughs or "moguls," which are the humps of sand in the surf zone. There are 2- to 3-foot guts in between them, and that's where the trout will be feeding. The waters off of Hilton Head and Turtle islands are productive. On really calm days, you may be able to sight fish. Big live baits under floating corks work well, as do topwater plugs and soft-plastic jigs. Areas where small creeks run out of the barrier islands are good places to start.

Charleston

Atlantic Ocean

Edisto Island

During the dead of winter, hardcore anglers target the sluggish fish in deeper holes.

NORTH CAROLINA

Area of Detail

Coastal North Carolina boasts vast sounds and complex river systems. The main features are the Cape Fear River basin, Pamlico Sound, Albemarle Sound, Bogue Sound, Croatan Sound, Currituck Sound and Roanoke Sound. All offer great trout water,

In late October, the only significantly migratory population of trout pours out of Chesapeake Bay waters, heads south, and runs up into Albemarle Sound feeder creeks and rivers.

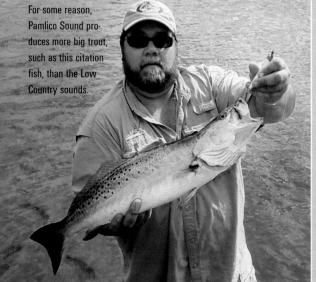

For some reason, Pamlico Sound produces more big trout, such as this citation fish, than the Low Country sounds.

although the fisheries suffer from gillnet pressure.

Migratory patterns of spotted seatrout in southern North Carolina are similar to trout movements throughout the Low Country. The fish move out toward the sounds and the mouths of the sounds in summer and find deepwater winter homes up creeks and rivers.

In winter, the sounds toward the northern extent of North Carolina waters also benefit from a push of fish migrating south out of Chesapeake Bay, and even parts north, to escape the cold. It's the only known body of seatrout that makes a relatively long migration.

Jacksonville

North Carolina

Wilmington

Cape Fear

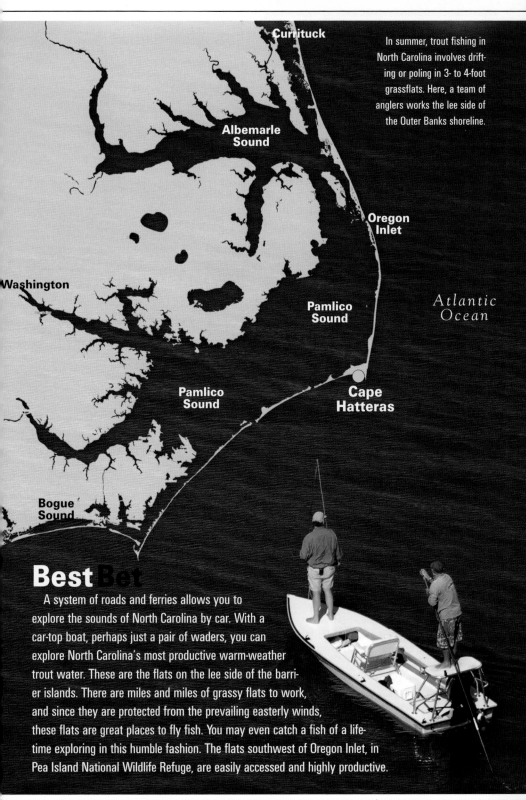

Currituck

Albemarle
Sound

In summer, trout fishing in
North Carolina involves drifting or poling in 3- to 4-foot
grassflats. Here, a team of
anglers works the lee side of
the Outer Banks shoreline.

Oregon
Inlet

Washington

Pamlico
Sound

*Atlantic
Ocean*

Pamlico
Sound

Cape
Hatteras

Bogue
Sound

Best Bet

A system of roads and ferries allows you to
explore the sounds of North Carolina by car. With a
car-top boat, perhaps just a pair of waders, you can
explore North Carolina's most productive warm-weather
trout water. These are the flats on the lee side of the barrier islands. There are miles and miles of grassy flats to work,
and since they are protected from the prevailing easterly winds,
these flats are great places to fly fish. You may even catch a fish of a lifetime exploring in this humble fashion. The flats southwest of Oregon Inlet, in
Pea Island National Wildlife Refuge, are easily accessed and highly productive.

VIRGINIA

Area of Detail

Chesapeake Bay has resident fish, but in the late spring, trout pour out of North Carolina's Albemarle Sound, migrate up the beach and deep into the Bay.

The Chesapeake Bay's seatrout fishery is mostly limited to late spring through late fall, and far more specks are caught in the lower Bay, in Virginia waters. That said, the Tangier Island area gets its share of fish in the warmer months.

May through October, the southern Chesapeake Bay offers great seatrout fish-

Working grass shorelines in the lower bay with streamer flies is a popular pursuit.

Virginia

ing. By November, most of the fish have migrated south into North Carolina sounds and up the Tarheel State's rivers.

Top areas include the Lynnhaven River (near Virginia Beach), Poquoson Flats (near Hampton, VA), Plantation Creek (Virginia's Eastern Shore) Hampton Roads Bridge Tunnel, Ocean View (in Norfolk), Little Creek Inlet, Lynnhaven Inlet and Rudee inlet. A few gators are also caught at the Chesapeake Bay Bridge Tunnel each fall.

In the fall, the surf near Virginia Beach and beaches south such as Sandbridge produce good catches both from the sand and from piers. In fact, Virginia offers some of the best rough-water surf fishing for trout on the Atlantic seaboard.

Best Bet

The best trout fishing generally occurs in the lower Chesapeake Bay, especially in the late spring and fall when the migrations occur. In the heat of summer, stick close to the inlets which allow cooler water into the bay during the incoming tide. Areas such as Long Creek, the Poquoson Flats, Back River, the Hampton Roads Bridge Tunnel, Rudee Inlet and the Elizabeth River get red-hot.

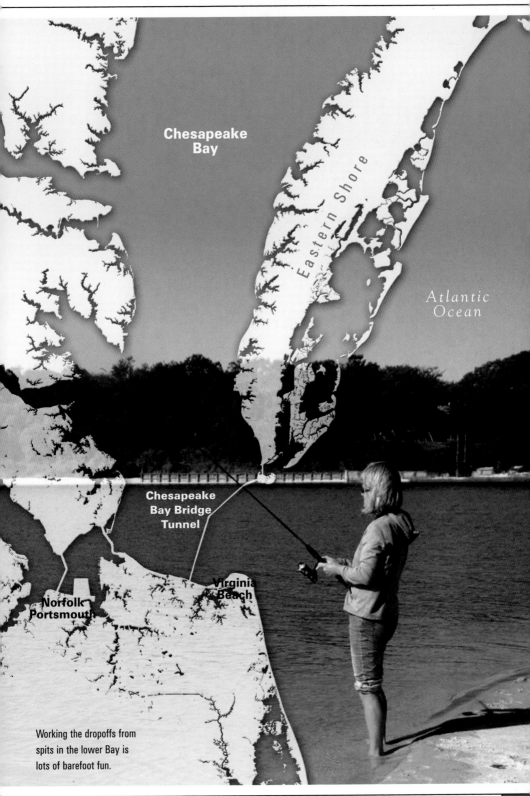

Chesapeake
Bay

Eastern Shore

Atlantic
Ocean

Chesapeake
Bay Bridge
Tunnel

Virginia
Beach

Norfolk
Portsmouth

Working the dropoffs from
spits in the lower Bay is
lots of barefoot fun.

CHAPTER 17

Tournaments and Records

There are hundreds of local inshore tournaments that are either dedicated trout tournaments or have trout divisions. There is no national "seatrout tour" or anything on par with the national redfish tournament series, but several "majors" occur each year for serious trout anglers. Winning or even placing in these tournaments adds to an inshore angler's cache. After all, in most states catching a gigantic trout still garners more prestige than a giant redfish or most other species. Big trout are often recognized as more elusive and difficult to catch. There is such a mystique surrounding them.

All states where trout occur keep state records, and some states offer awards, or citations, for trophy fish of a minimum weight.

The highest honor of all is setting a world record, or one of the line-class division records. World sportfishing records are administered by the International Game Fish Association, with headquarters in Dania Beach, Florida.

Several major tournaments are annual events, and hundreds of small local tournaments with trout divisions celebrate the fun of inshore fishing.

This angler used a relatively large topwater lure to avoid dinks and catch this tournament contender.

Tournaments

Tournaments often require anglers to bring trout back to a weigh station. Some are kill tournaments. Others require that you keep the fish alive in a release well. If the fish dies, the angler may be penalized. Points, ounces or pounds may be knocked off.

Increasingly, inshore tournaments require the angler to catch, measure and perhaps photograph their catch before releasing it on the spot. This format is best for local fish populations. Awards for sheer numbers of trout may also be given. Some tournaments require anglers to use artificial lures or flies only.

The Majors

The 73-year-old Miami Metropolitan South Florida Fishing Tournament, informally known as the "Miami Met," is one of the longest running tournaments in America and it has a seatrout division. For nearly eight decades, this tournament has fueled the popularity of competitive fishing, and offers an award for both the heaviest fish caught and heaviest fish in line class divisions. The event runs over the course of months.

Tournament anglers try to land trout quickly, due to their soft mouths. Below, the moment of truth at the weigh station.

Tournaments can be held to bring the angling community together out of shared passion and concern for the resource.

The State of Texas Angler's Rodeo (STAR) is another big-name tournament which spans the course of three months and the entire Texas coast. More than $1,000,000 in prizes is awarded. The tournament benefits the Coastal Conservation Association, which has won landmark victories in Texas, including gamefish status for seatrout, a net ban, and a dedicated stocking program. It also invests in the next generation of angler/conservationists. Prepaid college scholarships worth approximately $300,000 are awarded to kids each year, in increments up to $50,000 each, for catching the easiest and most plentiful bay species.

The STAR tournament is exclusive in that all tournament entrants must be current CCA Texas members. Fishing categories include: speckled trout, flounder, sheepshead, gafftop, dorado, king mackerel and ling (cobia). CCA Louisiana runs a similar event, with speckled trout competitions split into zones. In Alabama, the Alabama Deep Sea Fishing Rodeo, which began in the 1920s, offers a trout division.

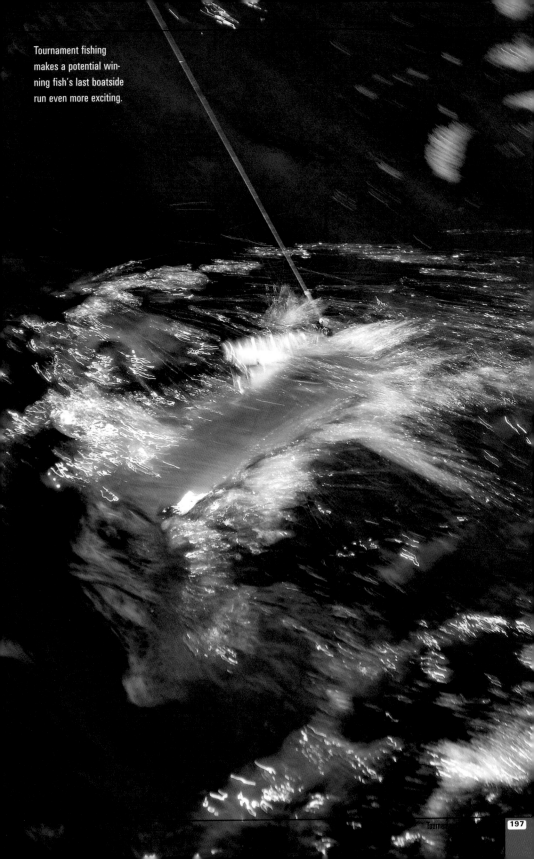

Tournament fishing makes a potential winning fish's last boatside run even more exciting.

And in Florida, the Destin Fishing Rodeo, which began in 1949, also has a "Pan Fry" division, which includes trout.

Arguably the most lucrative of trout fishing events is the Texas Trout Series, a 3-tournament mini-tour that has paid out as much as $10,000 to the winners, who are for the most part professional fishermen. Anglers must bring fish back alive to a weigh-in station. A penalty of 8 ounces is assessed if the fish is dead or injured. Winners must submit to a polygraph test to ensure that all tournament rules were followed.

Records and Line Testing

Most states keep track of record fish caught on various line classes, as does the International Game Fish Association, which administers world records. These

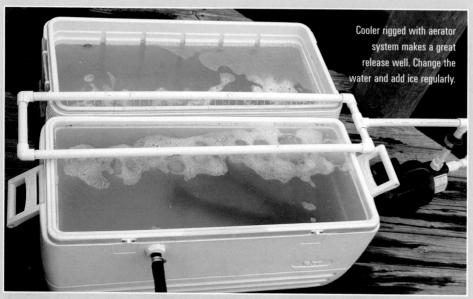

Cooler rigged with aerator system makes a great release well. Change the water and add ice regularly.

Advance Care

The experts at Bass Medics (www.bassmedics.com) offer some sage advice about keeping tournament fish alive. Fill the release well first thing in the morning, when surface temperatures are coolest, and do it in clean water, e.g. not at a marina. Another trick, in the warm months, is to put a handful of ice in the well every now and then. Try to keep well temps 8 to 10 degrees below surface water temps. Cool water increases the water's oxygen carrying capacity. Replace at least half of the water in the well every two to three hours. The fish-invigorating product Rejuvenade should be added according to directions. Some anglers also inject pure oxygen into the livewell. Finally, use water from the livewell, not from the water at the boat ramp or marina, when putting the fish in the weigh-in bag. SB

Serious tournament anglers add pure oxygen to release-well water.

entities publish a body of rules governing fair catches. These rules are extensive, but most begin with a philosophy of angling like the IGFA's, which states that "a fish captured that has not fought or has not had a chance to fight does not reflect credit on the fisherman." IGFA also has a separate division for fly fishing, and different body of rules. For a complete set of IGFA regulations, visit www.igfa.org.

Usually, the record applicant must weigh the catch on a certified scale. These days, some portable scales can be pre-certified. In the case of IGFA submissions, the angler must submit a segment of the line and leader if a leader was used. The line is then tested to see if it actually breaks at its advertised class. If you're serious about records, it's a good idea to test your line yourself before leaving the dock, especially if you're fishing with braided line. Keep in mind that braided gel-spun polyethylene and some hybrids test higher than monofilament. Your 8-pound-class may be forced to compete with the 12-pound division, for instance. SB

In 1987, Barbara Arthur caught this 11-pound, 11-ounce fish in Melbourne, Florida. It remains the Women's 16-pound-test line-class record.

Spotted Sea Trout State Records

Alabama: 12 pounds, 4 ounces

*Florida: 17 pounds, 7 ounces; Indian River Lagoon, Fort Pierce

Georgia: 9 pounds, 7 ounces; Christmas Creek, Cumberland Island

Louisiana: 12 pound, 10 ounces

Maryland: 16 pounds, 6 ounces; Roaring Point

Mississippi: 10 pounds, 6 ounces

New Jersey: 11 pounds, 2 ounces; Holgate surf

North Carolina: 12 pounds, 4 ounces; Wilmington

South Carolina: 11 pounds, 2 ounces; Murrells Inlet

Texas: 15.6 pounds; Lower Laguna Madre

Virginia: 16 pounds; Mason Beach

*World Record Seatrout

CHAPTER 18

Conservation

Sportsmen were America's original con-servationists. Recreational hunters did away with the practice of market hunting, which drove some game species such as the passenger pigeon into extinction and many others to the brink. That ethos led to the pro-tection of some fish species and waters from commercial exploitation.

The passion that anglers have for spotted seatrout and trout fishing has driven some of the most important precedents and reforms in fisheries and coastal management. But we are not, by any means, out of the woods. Anglers must still work to ensure that seatrout fish-eries around the country are managed sustain-ably, or better yet, optimally, and that the habi-tats essential to their success are protected and enhanced.

Speckled trout are an indicator species. Their abun-dance or lack thereof can signal estuary health or major problems. Given half a chance, trout will flourish.

Too much fresh water and trout eggs sink to the bottom and die. Water this dirty wreaks havoc throughout the ecosystem. Florida's St. Lucie River; June 2005.

WARNING

HIGH BACTERIA AND BLUE GREEN ALGAE LEVEL WARNING. AVOID CONTACT WITH WATER IN THE ST. LUCIE RIVER

MARTIN CO. HEALTH DEPT.

Conservation Cornerstones

Conservation begins with the individual angler. You can pitch in simply by purchasing fishing (and hunting) gear and marina fuel. In the 1930s, sportsmen went to Congress and actually asked to be taxed, provided that a portion of every sale of hunting or fishing merchandise goes to fund conservation programs. These excise tax funds are often used to buy coastal land and restore estuaries.

You can also pitch in by releasing your larger fish, handling the fish you intend to release carefully, and keeping only the number of fish you really need for dinner. Fishing with the "leave it as you found it" principle is another imperative. Take your

Florida's Indian River Lagoon: Martin County High School students replant native vegetation to stabilize sediments along important creek nursery habitats.

trash such as fishing line out with you, and make sure you don't damage habitats such as seagrass meadows with your propeller. At home, avoid using fertilizers which may find their way into coastal waters and encourage harmful algae blooms, including red tides. Washing your boat on the grass or other porous surface helps keep soaps and oils from entering the watershed, too.

Individual responsibility goes beyond on-the-water behavior. America's fisheries are a public trust resource, which means they belong to us as individual citizens and must be protected from special interests by private citizens.

individual ethics as the basis of conservation policy. It is hard to make a man, by

does not spring naturally from his own personal sense of right and wrong." —Aldo Leopold

Due to dramatically increasing coastal populations, development pressure and climate change, our coastal fisheries are under enormous stress. By joining a national conservation organization such as the Coastal Conservation Association, and fighting alongside neighbors to protect our coastal habitats from destruction, you can become a complete angler.

Captain Marcia Foosaner gently releases a big sow trout. Support the fish from underneath and revive until it swims off vigorously.

Fisheries Management

Spotted seatrout are prolific spawners, which makes them a relatively easy species to manage. Unless some dramatic environmental change stops them, trout spawn around the new and full moons each month from May through September. Sometimes spawning occurs as early as April and as late as October. In the two-week span between spawning events, females can generate from 250,000 to more than 1 million eggs, depending on the fish's size and health.

Cautious fishery management and habitat conservation/enhancement equal healthy trout populations.

Mangroves and oysters provide essential habitat and preserve water quality.

Rebuilding Reefs

You first must improve local water quality conditions enough for oysters to survive. Then partnerships between government, local environmental groups and scientists can lead to successful oyster restoration projects. In Florida, projects of note have occurred in Martin County, St. Lucie County and in Tampa Bay. Restoration efforts are ongoing in most regions where you find trout, including South Carolina, Georgia, Alabama, Mississippi, Louisiana, Texas and Chesapeake Bay.

Overfishing occurs when a species is harvested faster than it can reproduce itself. Fortunately, trout are not presently overfished by any official label anywhere in their range, which is a testament to their fecundity. Still, healthy trout stocks cannot be taken for granted. Managers must ensure that enough trout survive to reproduce or stocks will become overfished. Managers can also ensure healthy populations and trophy fish by limiting the take of large trout, which are the large females capable of generating a million eggs, every two weeks, for five months in a row. Protecting these fish also keeps the size genes in the population.

There are two key management measures which have helped seatrout populations in major regions more than any other reforms. The first is the decommercialization of the species in a majority of areas, and the second is the elimination of gill netting.

The state of Texas led the way on both counts, according no-sale status to trout in 1981 and completing a ban on commercial netting of all species in 1988. Florida, the largest of the trout states, accomplished its own ban of gill nets in '95 after a grassroots constitutional amendment campaign led not by state officials but by anglers. It was a historic victory for general public fishing that has had profound effects for dozens of species. Louisiana and Georgia are among other states outlawing the commercial entangling gear. Besides stopping gill nets, Florida has prohibited sales of trout during all but three summer months, and implemented strict size and bag limits on recreational catches. The end result is that populations of the species are considered to be higher than in a half-century or more. Of course, the issue of habitat degradation can be a recurring problem. SB

These sensitive coastal habitats had been abused by mining and other industrial uses. Volunteers helped clean up the area to prep for restoration.

1 week

Partnerships Work

Cockroach Bay is located in the southeast portion of Tampa Bay. The project has successfully restored 175 acres of wetlands. Thousands of volunteers worked to remove illegally dumped solid waste from the salterns and have planted native plant species in intertidal areas. Federal, state and local governments all participated in this effort with environmental groups, private industry, volunteer groups and educational facilities. Public support and the leveraging of resources made this a cost-effective restoration project that can be described as an example to the rest of the nation.

With the hydrology repaired, volunteers could replant native marsh grasses. They soon flourished.

6 months

Cockroach Bay is now a fully restored mosaic of habitats, including the marsh grasses so vital for juvenile fish.

1 year

Habitats and Water Quality

To mature and reproduce successfully, trout need a proper mix of fresh and salt water. Although they move out along beachfronts and occasionally to deeper offshore habitats, spotted seatrout are estuarine fish. Estuaries are mixing zones of fresh and salt water, brackish environments that are the nurseries for almost every non-pelagic saltwater organism that we understand well enough to value. The reason that you don't find trout on Bahamian flats or on Caribbean islands is a lack of fresh water.

Of course, too much fresh water, or excess nutrients, can be troublesome. Massive harmful discharges are frequent events in several key trout fisheries. These include the Mobile Delta, Chesapeake Bay, Florida's St. Lucie River/Indian River Lagoon estuaries and Florida's Caloosahatchee River/Pine Island Sound. Through the first half of the Twentieth century, the United States devoted considerable energy toward harnessing these and other waterways for navigation, flood control and irrigation. Protecting citizens and stimulating the economy were inarguably good intentions, but an unfortunate byproduct was the unraveling of estuarine systems. The billions of gallons of polluted water kill seagrasses and oyster reefs, and the direct result of this loss of essential habitat is decreased populations of gamefish such as trout. Fertilized trout eggs sink and die in water that is less than 15 parts per thousand salt. Depending on the duration of the discharges, a portion of an entire year class of trout may be lost.

Healthy estuaries produce bigger fish. Forage may be larger and more abundant, so trout can gain mass more quickly. The faster a fish

About the worst thing for trout is hundreds of billions of gallons of polluted agricultural runoff. The 2005 discharges, the latest to deluge the St. Lucie and Caloosahatchee River estuaries, destroyed critical habitats and disrupted spawning.

grows, the more likely it is to reach a ripe old age. Thus, healthy habitats and clean water allow trout to grow to optimal size, in optimal numbers, for optimal reproduction. It's imperative that we protect trout water from pollution and protect the habitats they depend on. SB

Ah, clear water, thick seagrass. Fishing as it should be.

Conservation Group Contacts

Texas Coastal Conservation Association: (800) 626-4222; www.ccatexas.org.

Louisiana Coastal Conservation Association: (225) 952-9200; www.ccalouisiana.com.

Mississippi Coastal Conservation Association: www.ccamississippi.org.

Alabama Coastal Conservation Association: (251) 478-3474; www.cca-alabama.org.

Florida Coastal Conservation Association: (407) 854-7002; www.ccaflorida.org.

Georgia Coastal Conservation Association: (912) 927-0280; www.ccaga.org.

South Carolina Coastal Conservation Association: (803) 865-4164; www.ccasouth carolina.com.

North Carolina Coastal Conservation Association: (919) 781-3474; www.ccanc.org.

Virginia Coastal Conservation Association: (757) 481-1226; www.ccavirginia.org.

Maryland Coastal Conservation Association: (888) 758-6580; www.ccamd.org.

Other Organizations

Chesapeake Bay Foundation: (888) SAVEBAY; www.cbf.org.

National Wildlife Federation and links to state affiliates: (800) 822-9919; www.nwf.org, or www.targetglobalwarming.org.

Gulf Restoration Network: (504) 525-1528; www.healthygulf.org.

Marine Fish Conservation Network: (866) 823-8552; www.conservefish.org.

Snook Foundation: (407) 302-5550; www.snookfoundation.org.

South Carolina Conservation League: (843) 723-8035; www.coastalconservationleague.org.

North Carolina Coastal Federation: (800) 232-6210; www.nccoast.org.

Water Keeper Alliance and links to local waterkeepers: (914) 674-0622; www.waterkeeper.org.

Rivers Coalition (Florida): (772) 225-6849; www.riverscoalition.org.

PURRE Water Coalition (Caloosahatchee watershed, Florida): (239) 275-7872; www.purre.org.

CHAPTER 19

Tasty Trout

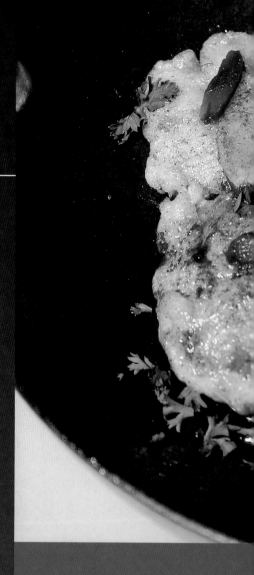

Seatrout are a popular table fish with fine-grained fillets that can be prepared in myriad ways. Trout tend to be sweeter in the cooler months especially in their northernmost range. Some anglers are of the opinion that they get a little soft and muddy tasting in Florida's Indian River Lagoon and in southwest Florida during the warmer months. Some trout may have worms embedded in the flesh along the backbone. These "spaghetti" caryophyllum worms are larval stages of a tapeworm that can only reach maturity in sharks, and don't survive in humans when eaten raw. The worms can easily be removed during filleting to make the meat more appealing.

Care of the fish between landing and the skillet is important. Keep fish and fillets cold. The fine-grained meat loses quality rapidly if left unchilled.

It's hard to beat fried trout fillets. But you can prepare trout in as many ways as any flaky, white-fleshed fish. Take care of your catch, and it will take care of your taste buds.

A stringer is an indispensable tool when kayaking or wading, but you may wind up sharing with a shark.

Clean Living

The term "put 'em on ice" isn't exactly accurate. Bury your trout in ice and keep draining the cooler.

There's an elemental sense of satisfaction in bringing home a fresh fish dinner. Bag limits range from conservative to quite liberal depending on which region you fish. But there are some things you can do to ensure your local trout populations remain strong.

Trout are a species that can be harvested at relatively high levels and enjoyed by anglers and their families.

First, keep only the fish you need for a fresh fish dinner. Trout flesh is soft and doesn't freeze well so it loses flavor easily.

Second, avoid killing big trout; they are mostly females which comprise a minority of the population. You can also avoid killing females by taking the fish that make the drum sound in your hand. These are males—female trout don't drum. Yes, you do get some strong silent types, but the majority of male trout drum when handled.

Third, respect these wild animals and your palate by taking care of your catch.

Finally, most states require you to keep your catch whole until you return to the boat ramp. In Florida, and some other places, pier, surf and wade fishermen are required to keep the catch whole, as well. Law enforcement officers need to be able to identify the species and make sure the individuals are within the slot limits. Check local regulations before you head out.

Cold and Clean

The colder you keep your seatrout throughout the day, the better those fish will taste. Do not skimp on the ice. You need enough ice to keep your catch completely covered. Drain the water as it melts, because fresh water can make the flesh soggy. Better yet, add seawater to the ice to create a super-chilled slurry. When you clean the fish, the flesh should be cold enough that it stings your fingers.

When cleaning trout, make sure you have a clean, flat surface that won't dull your knife. Wood or fiberglass cutting boards are best. Leave all but the fish you're working on in the cooler, unless it's chilly outside.

Trout are easy to clean and can be cleaned in a few ways. For those who like to fry, bake or broil fish whole, gut and behead the fish. Some connoisseurs remove the viscera but leave the head on. Make an incision at the anal vent and slice the length of the underbelly. Then reach in and remove viscera. Remove the head as well, if you like, but keep in mind that there's a fair amount of meat above the gills. Leave the skin on.

If you prefer filleting fish, try not to puncture the viscera, which gets bodily fluids on the flesh. Also avoid setting the fillet flesh-side down in slime. One way to avoid this is to always begin the fillet from the head. Slice an outline through the skin down both sides of the fillet, and move the knife gently along the backbone while lifting the flesh. You can cut out the rib cage as you fillet the fish if you work surgically. Don't cut the fillet all the way off the body. Stop at the end of the tail, leaving the skin attached to the tail. Then flip the fillet over so that it lies stretched out and skin-down between the forks in the tail. Then begin skinning the fillet where the skin is still attached to the tail. Use the hand that is not doing the cutting to pull the skin against the direction of the knife. Trout skin is very soft, so you don't want a super-sharp knife. It

should be reasonably sharp and sharpened evenly along the length of the blade so the skin doesn't catch on a dull section. Larger fillets can be sliced into chunks, which are especially good for deep frying.

Rinse the fillets in a minimal amount of cool fresh water, or, if available, clean salt water. The less fresh water that touches the fillets, the better they will taste.

Cleaning Techniques

Trout are easy to clean. Clean your fish according to how you intend to prepare it. You may want to gut, behead and scale the fish for baking or frying whole. Fillets work for a variety of dishes.

Make an incision behind the gill plate, then turn the knife "south."

Fillet close to the backbone to the tail, but do not cut the skin.

Flip the fillet over and begin lifting the meat off the skin.

Be sure to cut out the rib cage and any bones along the center line.

Recipes

Cooking up your catch is the way to consummate your day on the water. The sea's neat, let's eat.

Spotted seatrout have been a staple since pre-Columbian times. Today, each region adds its own flavor to seatrout dishes. You can bet on a spicy plate of sautéed fish in Texas and Louisiana. Frying trout is a family tradition throughout the South. Ceviche is very much in vogue. And trout can be gussied up in various gourmet styles, including trout amandine or pecan trout, in gumbos and even in lasagna. Here are a few favorites of the staff at *Florida Sportsman*.

Deep frying is a failsafe favorite way to prepare trout.

Panko-fried Trout

4 fillets of seatrout, about 4 ounces each
½ cup flour
12 ounces of cold beer
½ cup Panko (Japanese wheat flower) or Italian bread crumbs

Put ¼ inch of vegetable oil or peanut oil in a pan and get it HOT! You know the oil is hot enough when a dab of flour floats to the top deep-fried instantly. Dredge fillets in flour. Drop fillets in ice cold effervescent beverage such as beer. Roll fillets in Panko or Italian bread crumbs and cook until golden-brown on both sides. Don't

overcook the fillets, or they get dry with a strong fishy flavor. Keep in mind that meat keeps cooking well after you remove it from the heat source. The double dip is the secret to fluffy fried fish with a crunch. Serve with lemon juice, tartar or cocktail sauce. Serves 2.

Corn Meal Batter Fried Speckled Trout

6 to 8 fillets
¼ cup yellow corn meal
½ cup regular flour
¾ teaspoon baking powder
1 egg
½ teaspoon salt pepper (optional)
1 cup of ice cold water
Peanut oil
Cut trout fillets into small pieces or strips.

Mix corn meal, flour, baking powder, salt, pepper, water and egg. Blend well. Combine fish with batter; let soak if possible. Cook in about 1 inch of peanut oil until golden brown. Serve with lemon, tartar or cocktail sauce if desired. Serves 4.

Baked Seatrout

Serving Size: 1 or 2 fish per person, whole, scaled gutted and beheaded.
8 to 10 ounces of Italian dressing
1 cup butter
Salt & pepper
¼ cup chopped onion tops
2 cloves garlic, minced
1-2 medium onion(s), sliced
2 medium tomatoes, sliced

Preheat oven to 350 degrees. Place trout and dressing in shallow pan. Salt and pepper to taste. Place onions and tomatoes on top of trout; sprinkle with onion tops and garlic. Dot with butter. Bake approximately 20 to 30 minutes. Watch carefully to avoid burning onions and tomatoes; baste if necessary to prevent dryness.

Trout Amandine

4 fillets, about 4 ounces each
1 lemon
½ cup flour
½ stick butter
Salt and pepper
½ cup slivered almonds
2 tbsp. chopped parsley
¼ cup white wine

Sprinkle trout fillets with salt and pepper to taste. Squeeze lemon over both sides of the fillets, then coat fillets with flour. Melt butter at medium-high heat in a large non-stick pan. Add the fillets and cook for two or three minutes until lightly browned (lift edge with plastic spatula to check). Turn and cook another couple of minutes. Place fillets on paper towels. Brown the almonds, add the chopped parsley and stir. Add the wine and stir well, scraping bottom of pan to deglaze. Turn off heat, return fillets to pan and hold until ready to serve, then transfer fillets to a platter and pour the sauce and almonds over them. Serves 2.

Louisiana Stuffed Trout

16 speckled trout fillets
¼ cup melted butter
½ cup butter
½ cup chopped onion
½ cup chopped green onions
1 pound crab meat, picked to remove all shells
¼ pound shrimp, peeled
¾ cup bread crumbs
Salt and red pepper to taste
½ cup butter
¼ cup chopped celery
¼ cup chopped green onions
¼ cup chopped onions
2 cloves garlic, minced
¾ pound shrimp
¼ pound fresh mushrooms, sliced
¼ cup white wine

To prepare stuffing, sauté onions and celery in butter. Add crab meat and shrimp and simmer, uncovered, until shrimp is cooked, about 5 to 8 minutes. Add bread crumbs to thicken mixture. Add salt and red pepper to taste.

Butter two 9 x 13-inch baking dishes. Preheat oven to 350 F. Place 4 trout fillets in each and top with a scoop of stuffing, topped by another trout fillet. Drizzle melted butter on top. Bake for 30 to 40 minutes until fish is done.

While fish is baking, prepare sauce by melting butter and sauteing celery, green onions, onions and garlic. Add shrimp and simmer until pink. Add mushrooms and white wine. Simmer for 3 to 5 minutes. Arrange trout on serving platter and pour sauce over fish. Some of the sauce may be reserved and served in a gravy boat. Serves 8-10.

Seatrout Ceviche

3 pounds fresh speckled trout
6 limes
3 to 4 tomatoes, chopped
3 to 5 jalapeños, seeded and chopped
1 large onion, chopped
¼ to ½ bunch cilantro, chopped
1 garlic clove, chopped
2 tablespoons olive oil
Salt and black pepper, to taste

Cut fish into ½-inch cubes. Marinate and chill fish at least 4 hours in juice of 3 limes. Pour off liquid. Mix in remaining ingredients except limes. Squeeze juice of remaining limes on top. Serve with fresh tostadas or in chilled avocado halves. Serves 10-12. SB

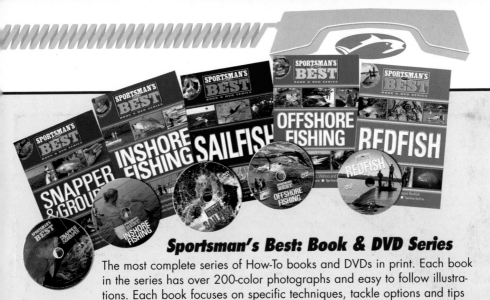

TROUT DVD

Sportsman's Best: Trout DVD brings the pages of this book to life. Join author Terry Gibson and the editors of *Florida Sportsman* and *Shallow Water Angler* as they travel throughout trout country. We'll show you tackle, tips and tactics to help you catch one of America's most popular inshore gamefish.

FEATURES

► THE SOUTH'S FAVORITE GAMEFISH
► RODS AND REELS
► LINES AND LEADERS
► IMPORTANT GEAR
► BOATS
► STRUCTURE
► ARTIFICIAL LURES
► SHRIMP
► RIGGING
► WADING
► AND MUCH, MUCH MORE!

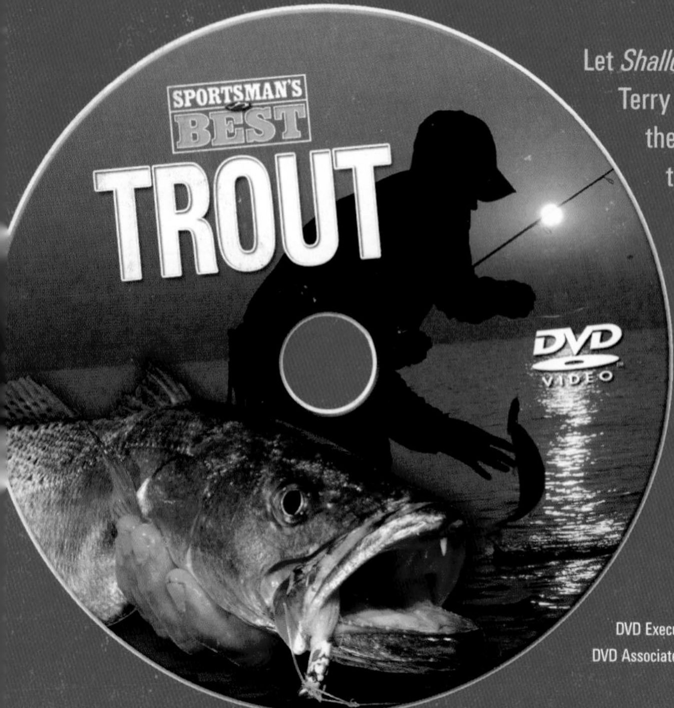

SPORTSMAN'S BEST
TROUT
DVD VIDEO

Let *Shallow Water Angler* Managing Editor Terry Gibson be your guide to some of the hottest seatrout fishing areas in the U.S. In this DVD, learn the basics of seatrout fishing such as proper tackle setups, but also hard-to-master techniques like natural bait rigging and how to work the most effective artificial baits. There's no better way of learning a new fishery, or tactic, than by seeing it done in a well-produced video.

DVD Executive Producer: Paul Farnsworth
DVD Associate Producer: Matt Weinhaus